EASY PIANO

FIRST 50 MOVIE THEMES

YOU SHOULD PLAY ON THE PIANO

T0039488

ISBN 978-1-5400-2965-2

HAL•LEONARD®

Visit Hal Leonard Online at
www.halleonard.com

Contact us:
Hal Leonard
7777 West Bluemound Road
Milwaukee, WI 53213
Email: info@halleonard.com

In Europe, contact:
Hal Leonard Europe Limited
42 Wigmore Street
Marylebone, London, W1U 2RN
Email: info@halleonardeurope.com

In Australia, contact:
Hal Leonard Australia Pty. Ltd.
4 Lentara Court
Cheltenham, Victoria, 3192 Australia
Email: info@halleonard.com.au

CONTENTS

AN AMERICAN SYMPHONY
from MR. HOLLAND'S OPUS

Composed by
MICHAEL KAMEN

Heroically

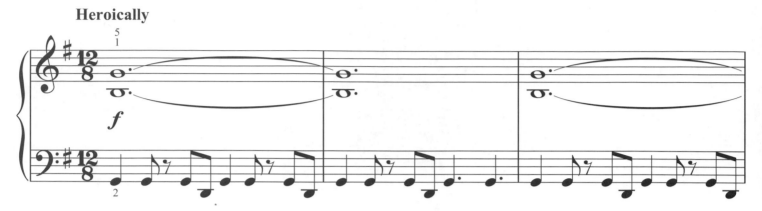

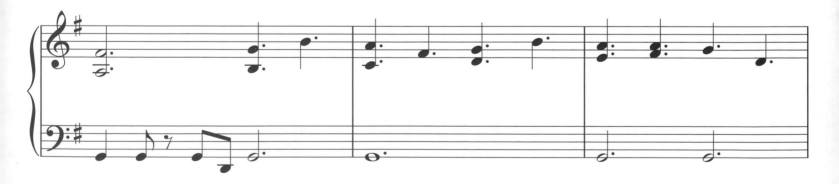

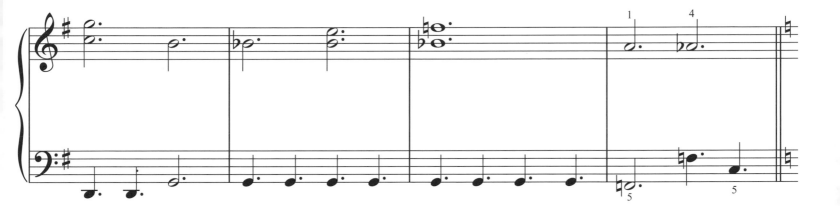

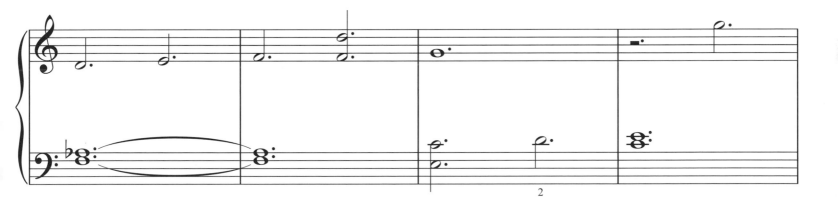

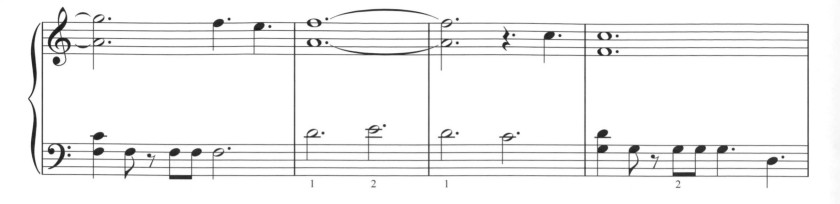

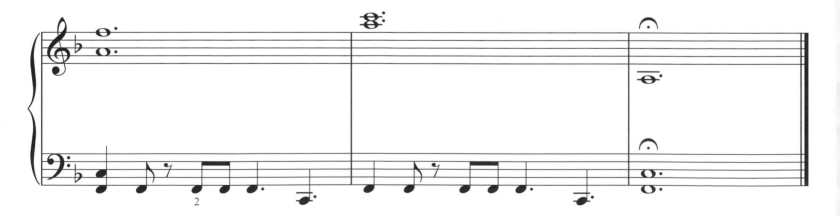

BELLA'S LULLABY

from the Summit Entertainment film TWILIGHT

By CARTER BURWELL

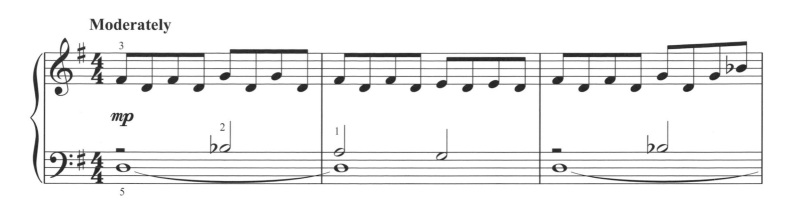

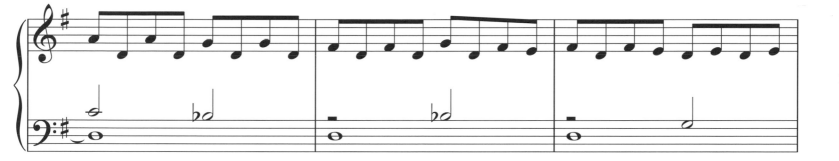

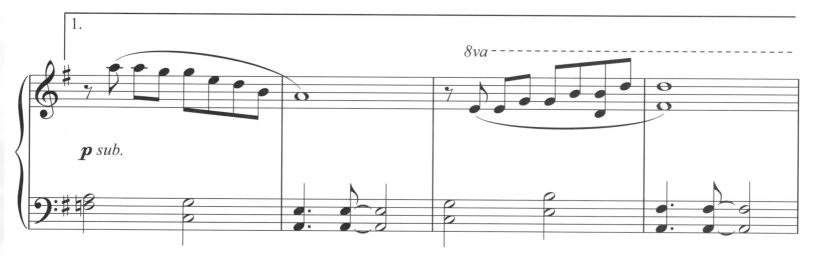

BRIAN'S SONG
Theme from the Screen Gems Television Production BRIAN'S SONG

Music by MICHEL LEGRAND

Moderately, with expression

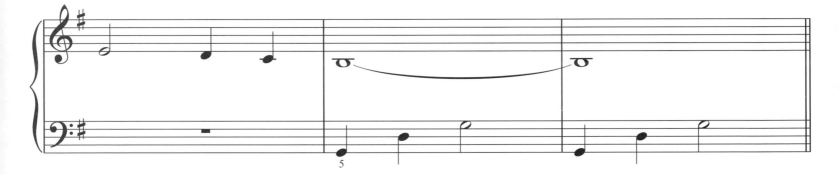

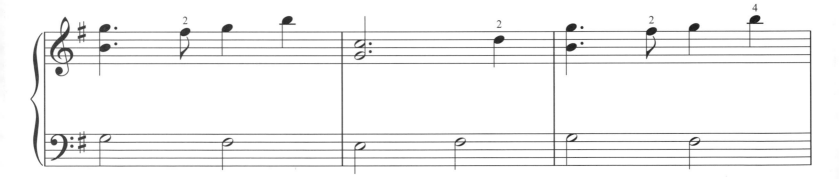

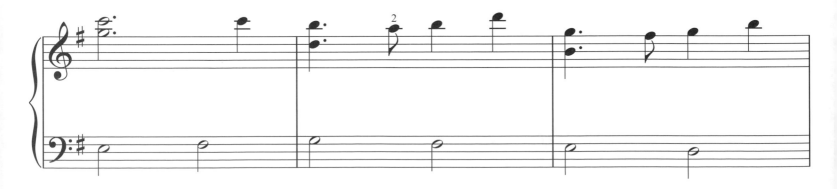

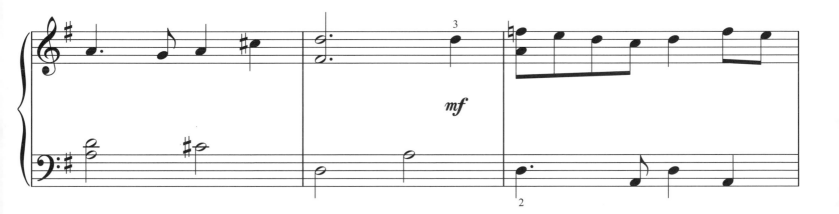

mf

CINEMA PARADISO

from CINEMA PARADISO

By ENNIO MORRICONE
and ANDREA MORRICONE

Moderately slow, with feeling

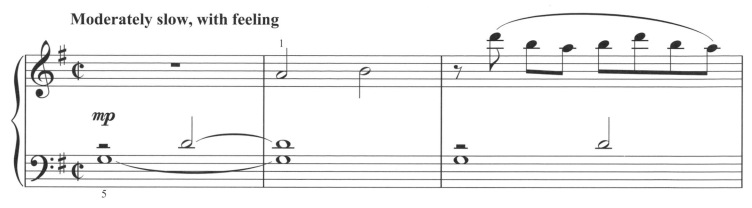

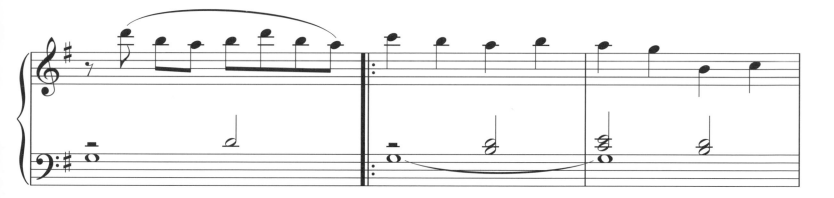

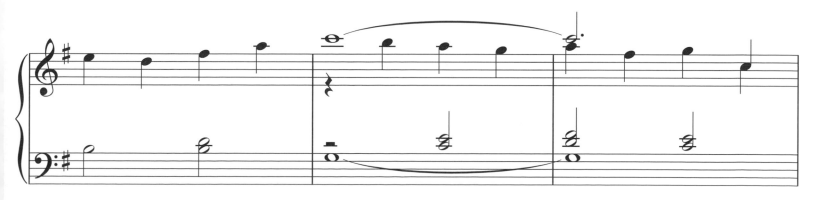

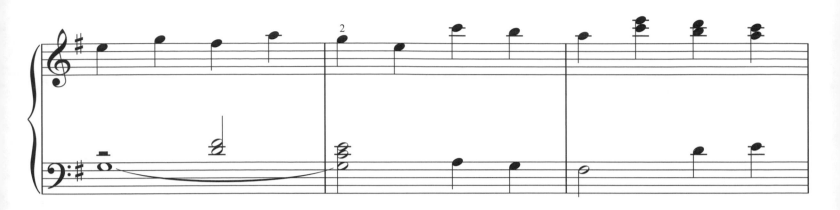

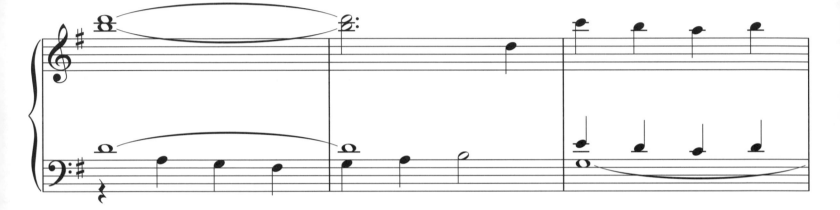

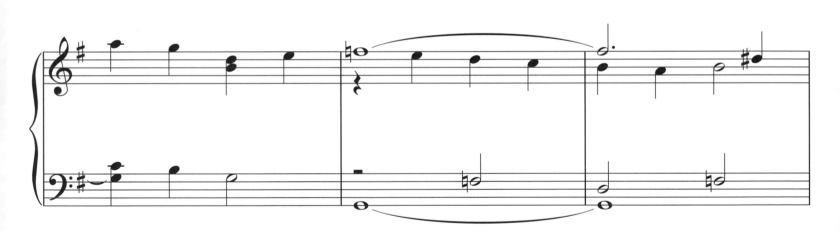

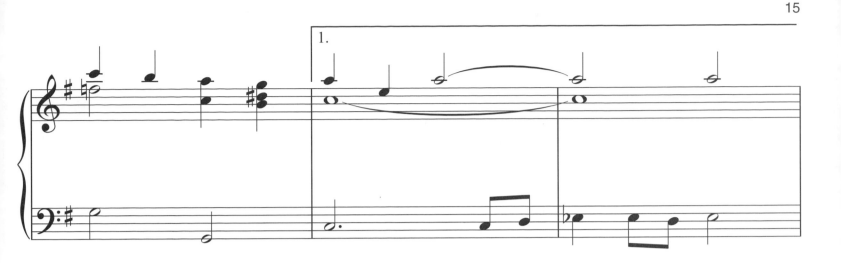

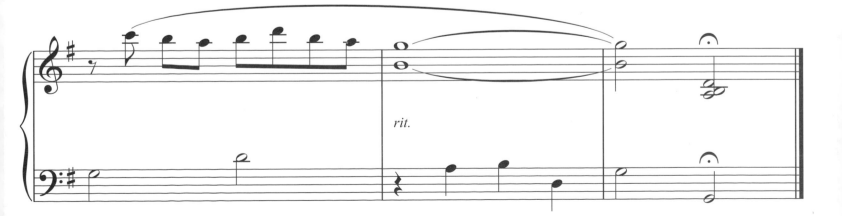

THE CHAIRMAN'S WALTZ
from MEMOIRS OF A GEISHA

By JOHN WILLIAMS

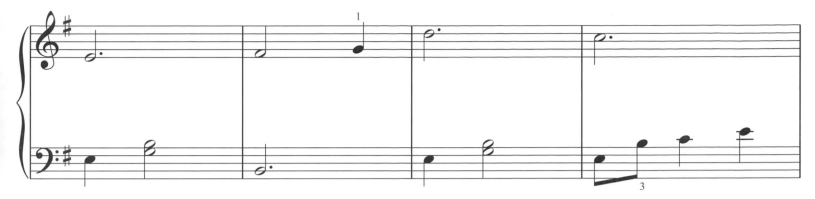

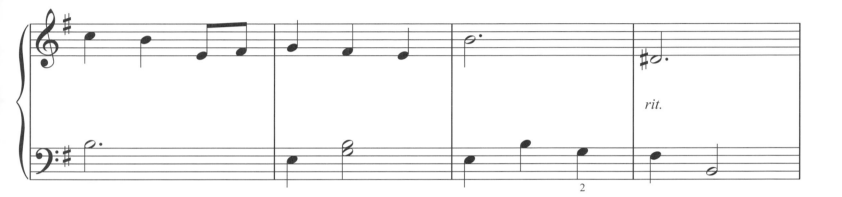

19

CHOCOLAT
(MAIN TITLES)
from the Motion Picture CHOCOLAT

By RACHEL PORTMAN

Slowly, with expression
Play both hands 8va

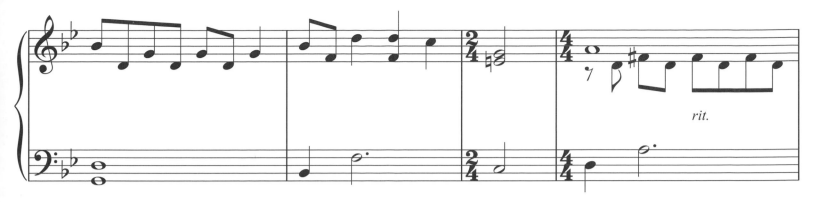

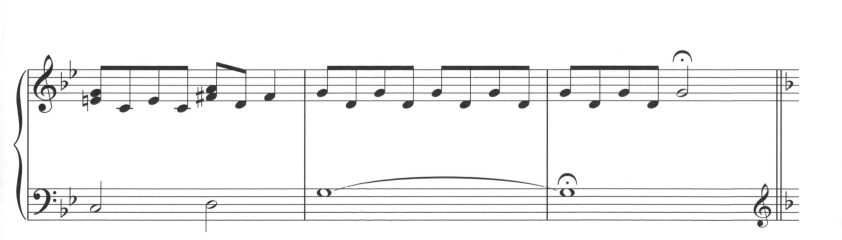

Moderately, in 2

Both hands as written

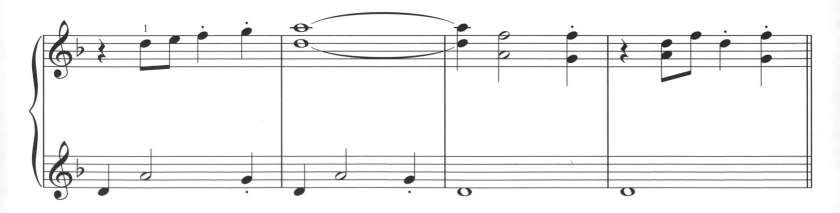

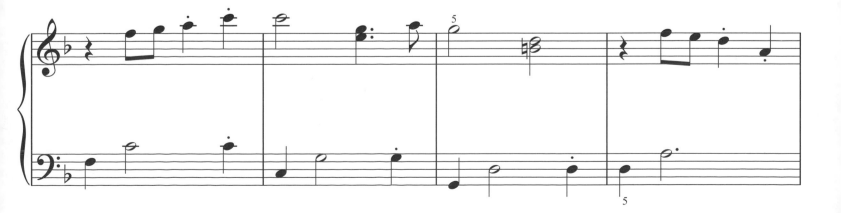

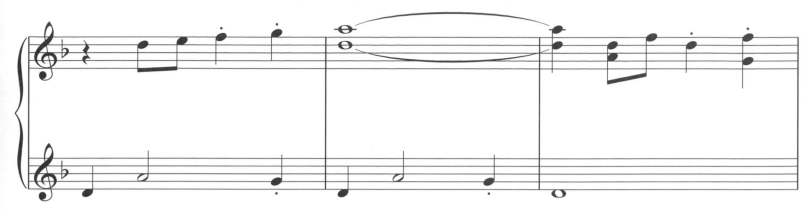

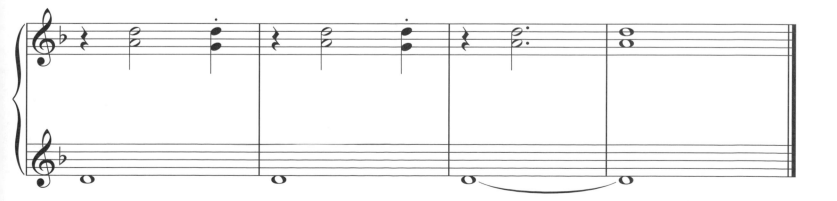

THE CLOCKS
from the Paramount Motion Picture HUGO

By HOWARD SHORE
Contains an excerpt from "AUBADE CHARMEUSE"
By JEAN PEYRONNIN

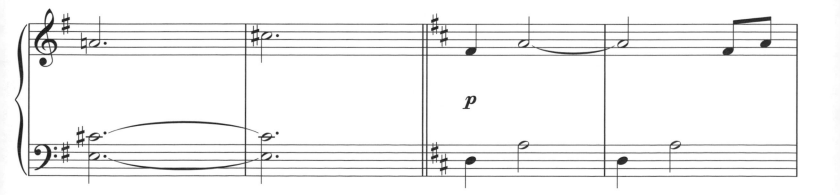

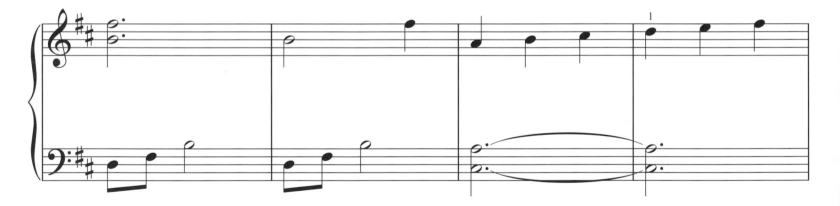

Slightly faster

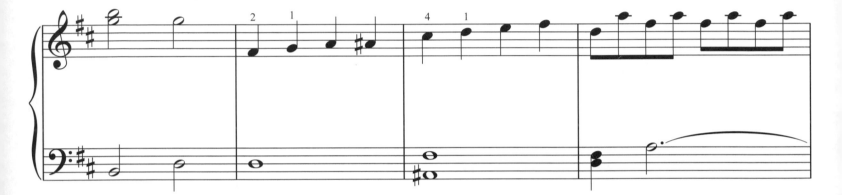

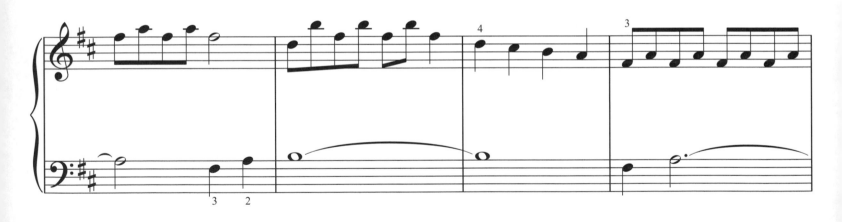

CONCERNING HOBBITS
from THE LORD OF THE RINGS: THE FELLOWSHIP OF THE RING

By HOWARD SHORE

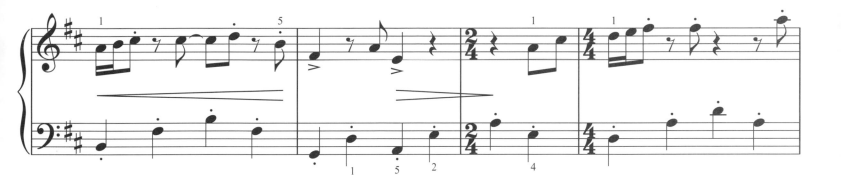

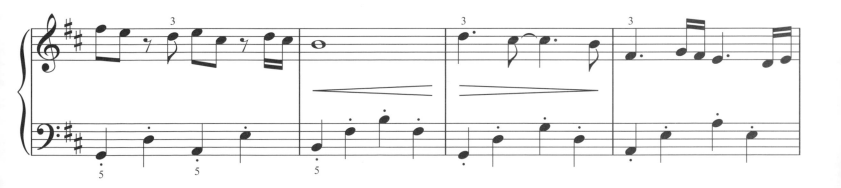

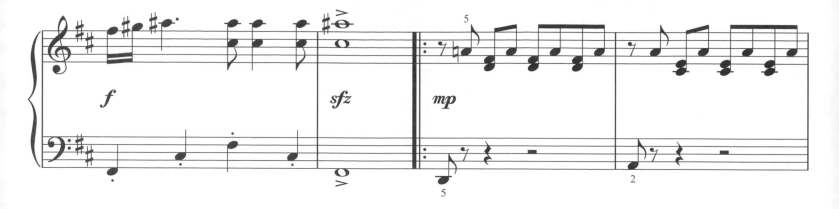

DAWN
from PRIDE AND PREJUDICE

By DARIO MARIANELLI

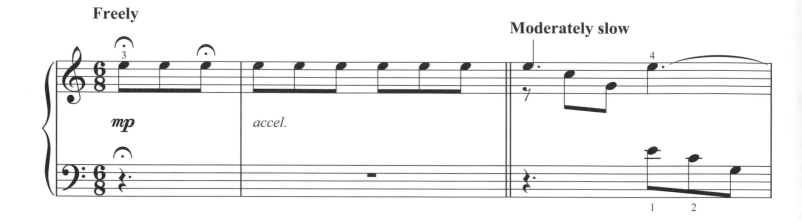

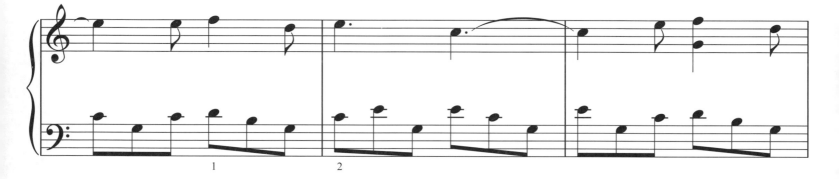

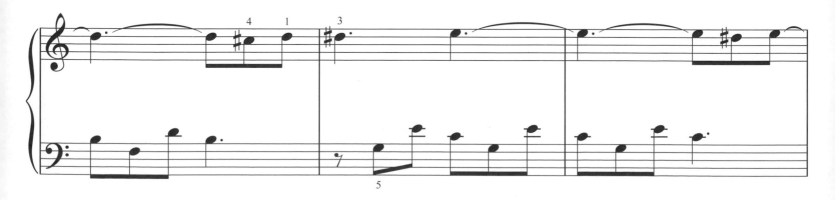

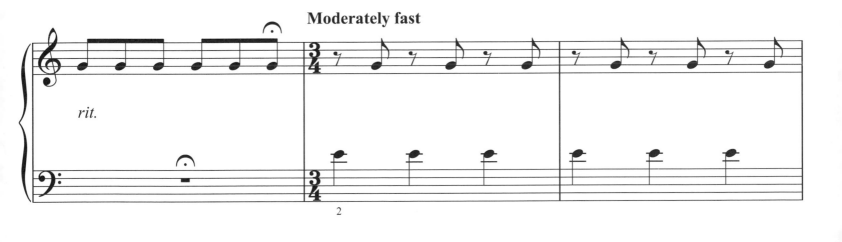

Moderately fast

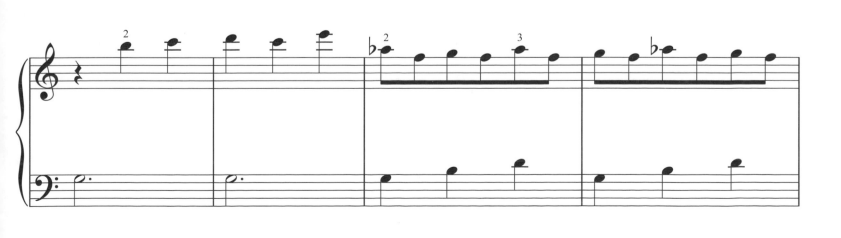

Slightly slower

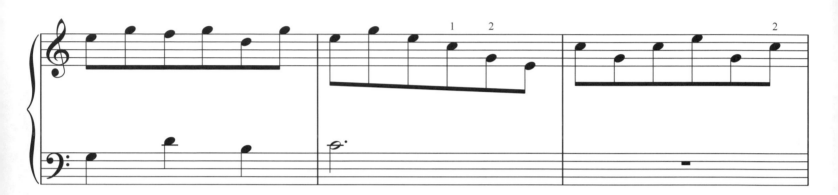

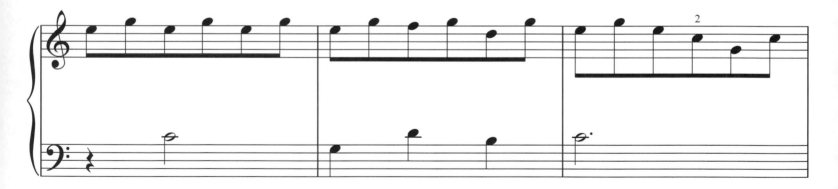

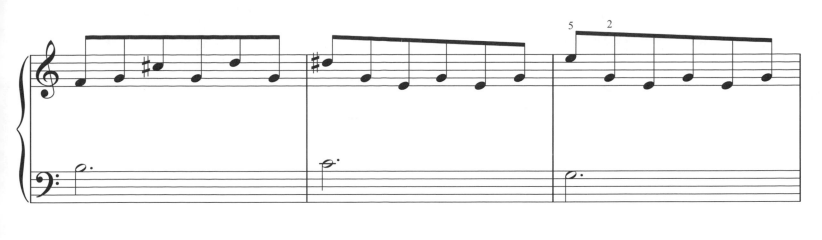

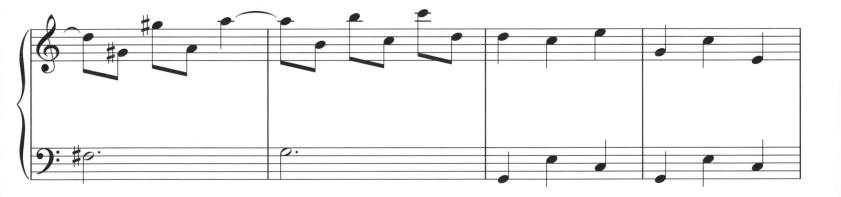

LOVE THEME FROM "FLASHDANCE"

from the Paramount Picture FLASHDANCE

Music by GIORGIO MORODER

Moderately slow

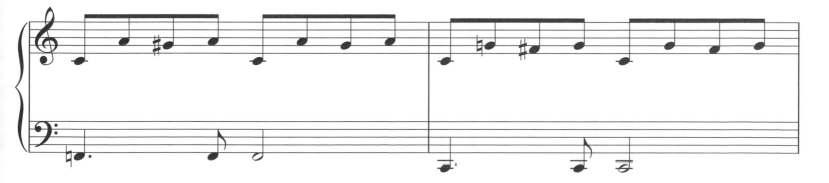

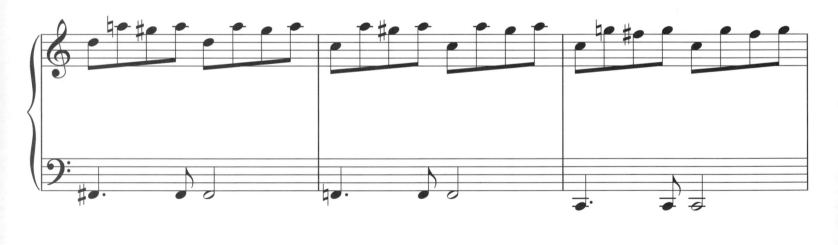

43

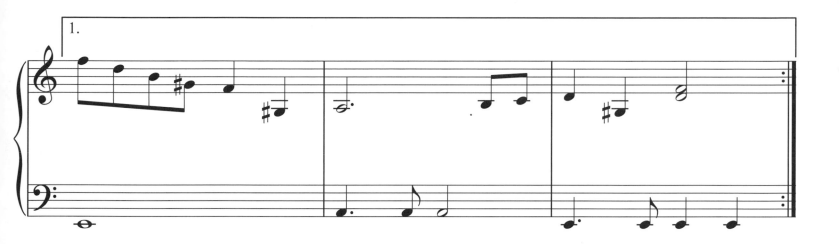

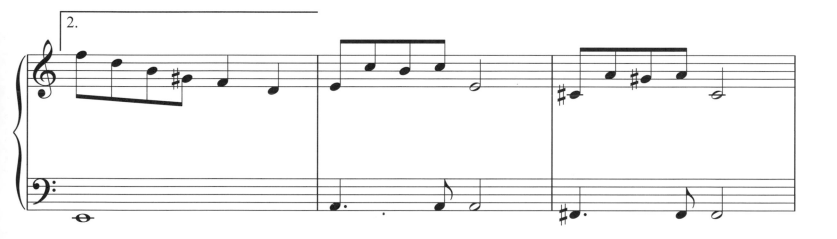

THE ENGLISH PATIENT
from THE ENGLISH PATIENT

Written by
GABRIEL YARED

With expression and rhythmic freedom

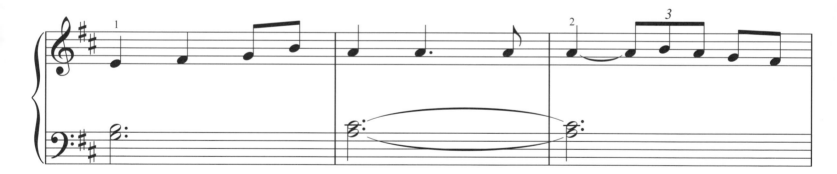

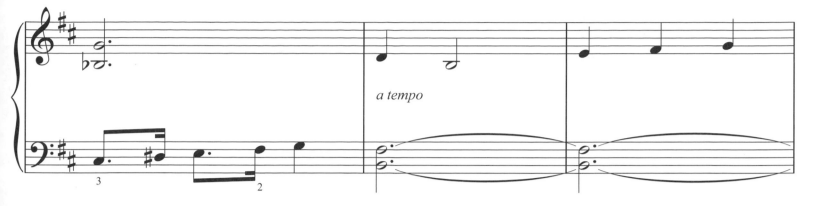

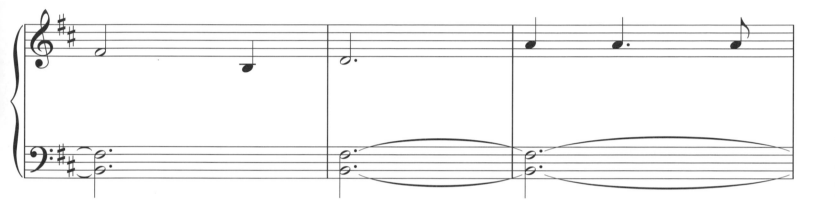

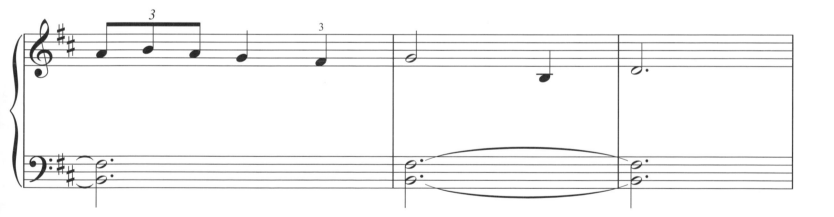

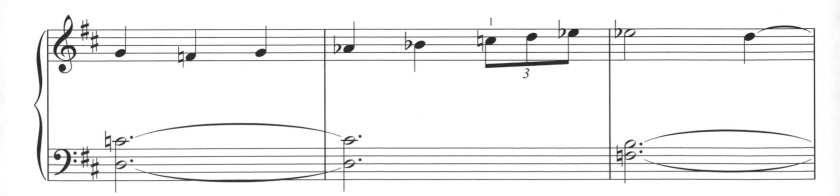

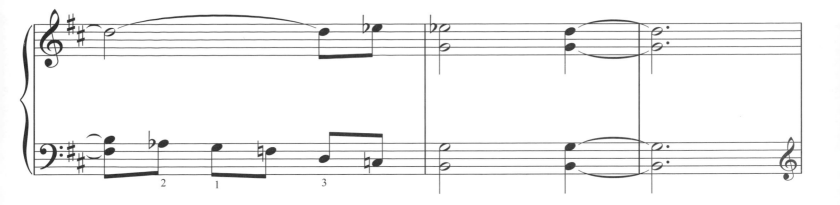

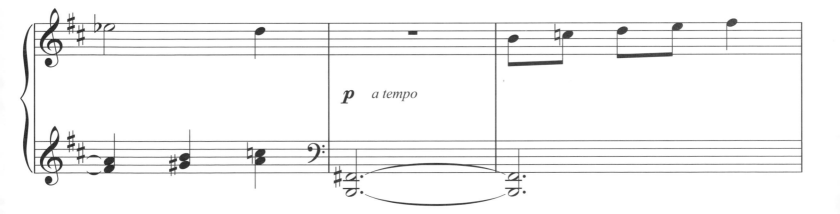

FORREST GUMP – MAIN TITLE
(Feather Theme)
from the Paramount Motion Picture FORREST GUMP

Music by
ALAN SILVESTRI

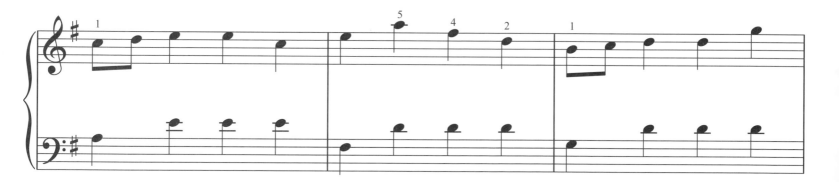

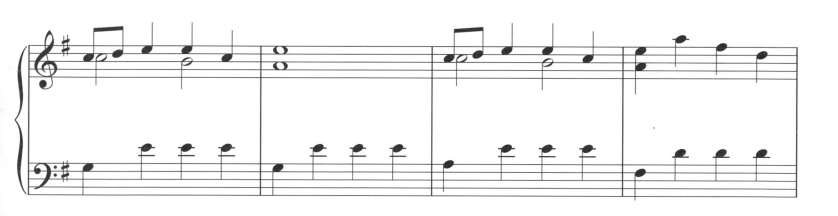

molto cresc.

f

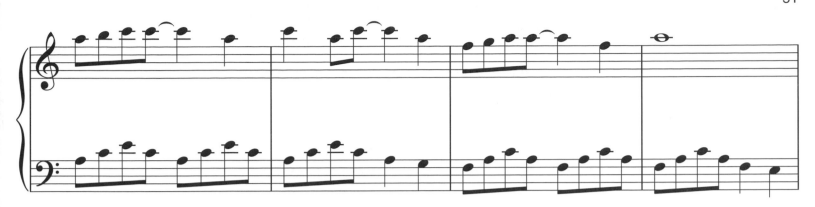

GABRIEL'S OBOE
from the Motion Picture THE MISSION

Music by
ENNIO MORRICONE

Slowly, expressively

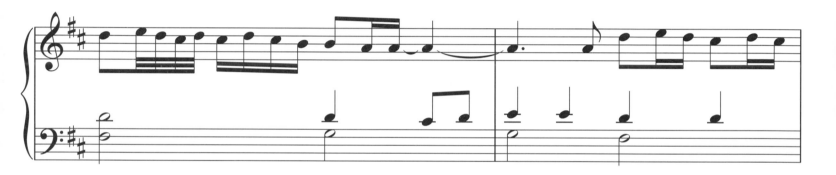

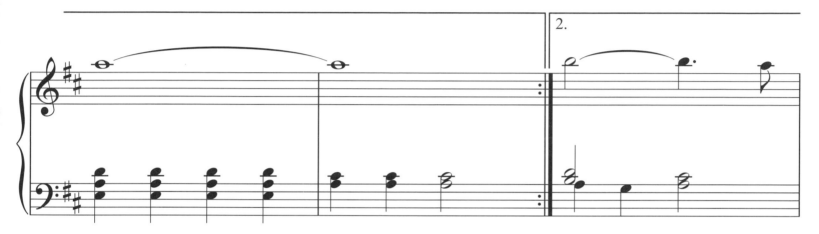

GALE'S THEME
(Main Title)
from THE RIVER WILD

By JERRY GOLDSMITH

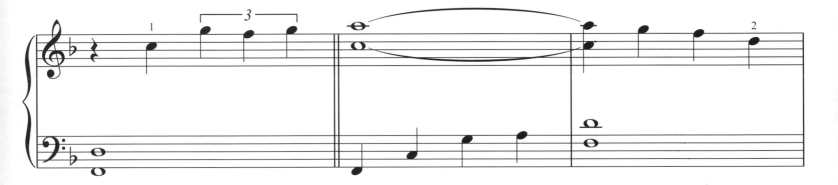

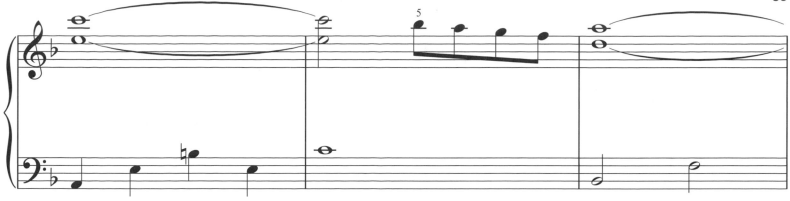

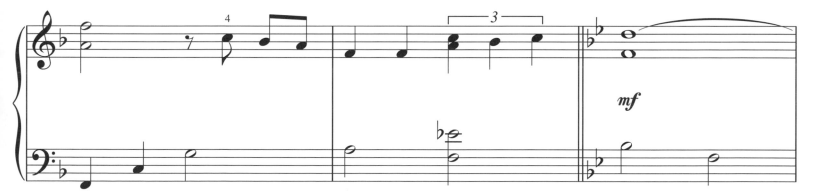

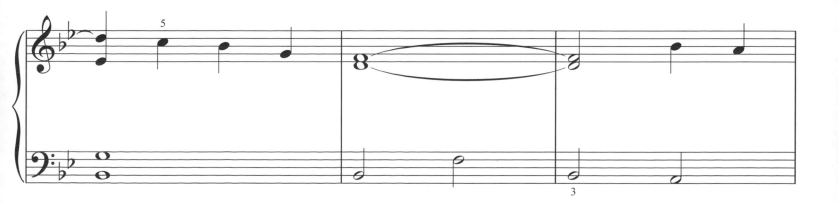

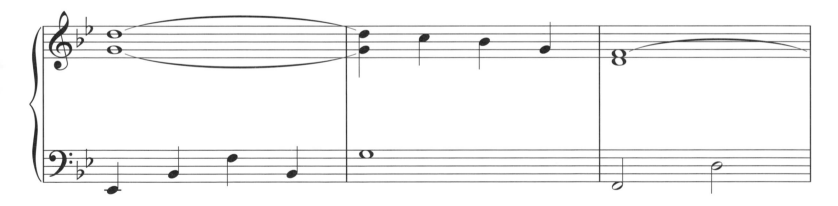

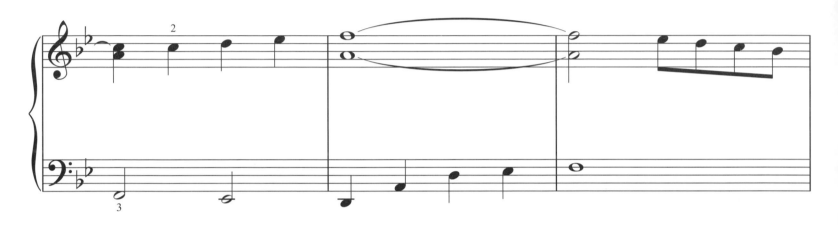

GLASGOW LOVE THEME
from LOVE ACTUALLY

Words and Music by
CRAIG ARMSTRONG

Slowly, very freely

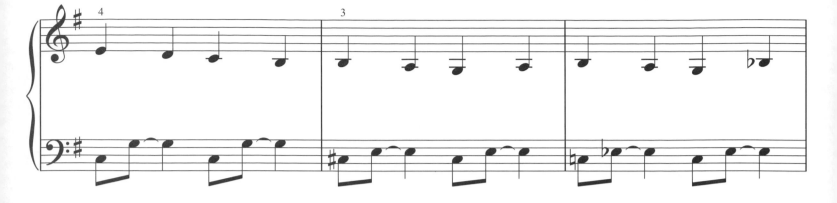

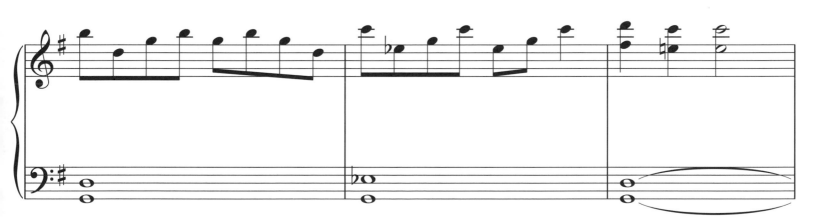

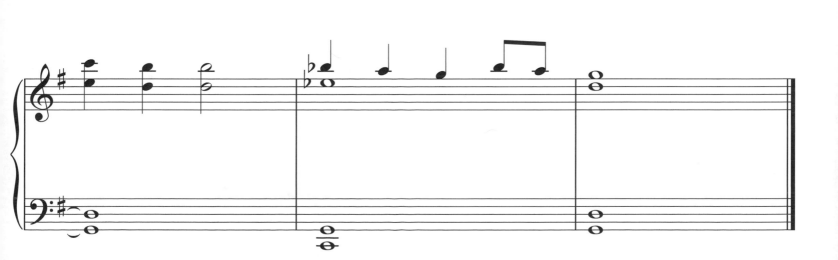

THE GODFATHER

(Love Theme)

from the Paramount Picture THE GODFATHER

By NINO ROTA

Slowly, with expresison

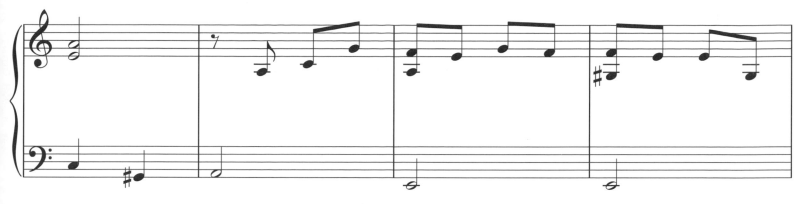

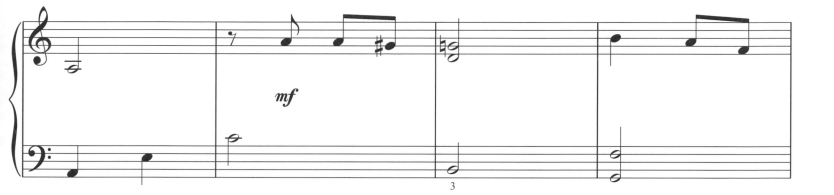

GOLDFINGER

from GOLDFINGER

Music by JOHN BARRY
Lyrics by LESLIE BRICUSSE
and ANTHONY NEWLEY

Moderately

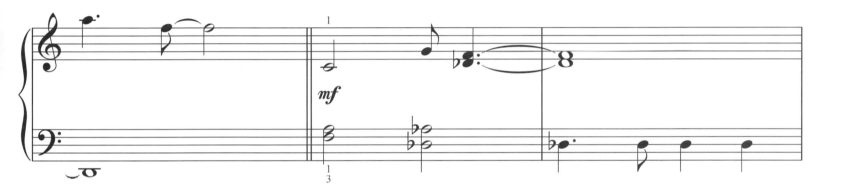

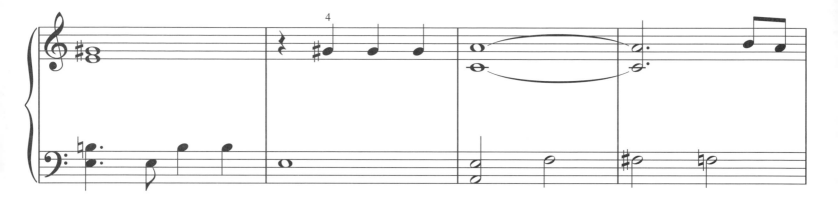

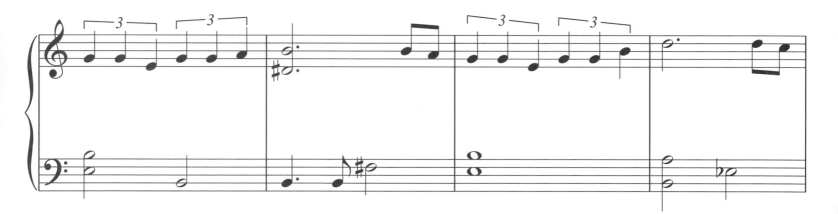

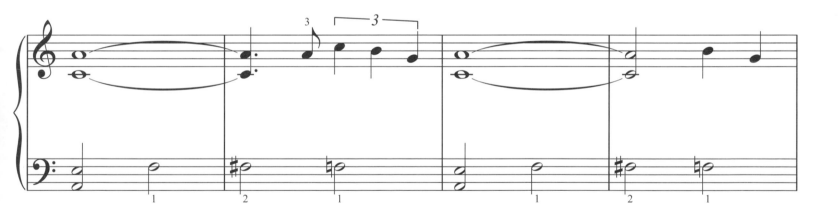

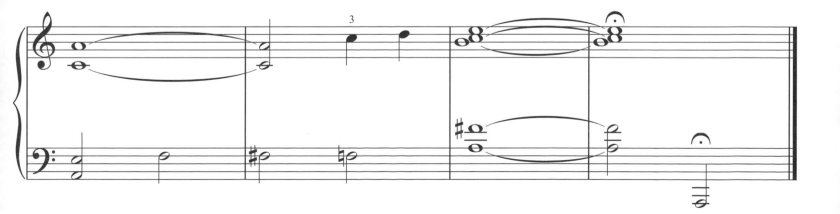

THE GUNS OF NAVARONE
from THE GUNS OF NAVARONE

Words and Music by DIMITRI TIOMKIN
and PAUL WEBSTER

Moderately

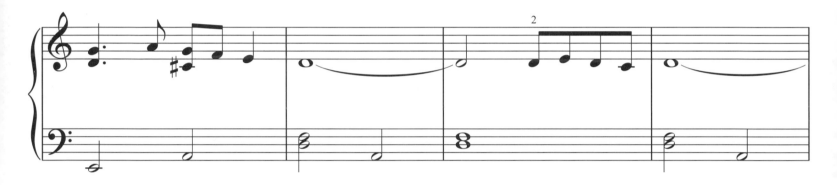

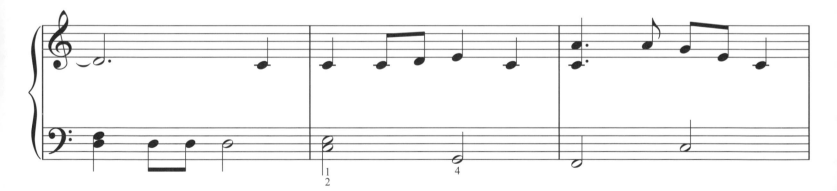

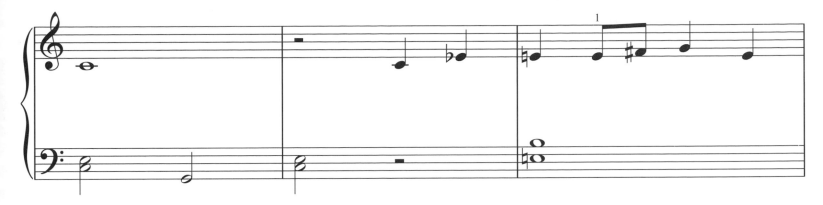

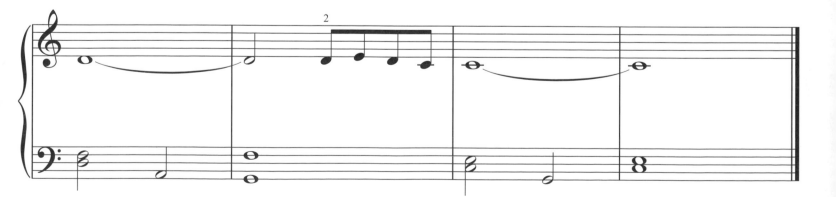

THE HEART ASKS PLEASURE FIRST
from THE PIANO

By MICHAEL NYMAN

Flowing

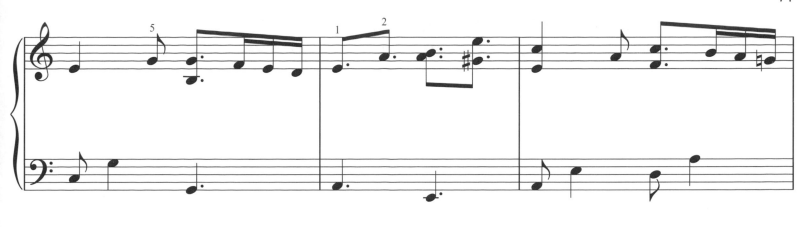

72

HE'S A PIRATE

from PIRATES OF THE CARIBBEAN: THE CURSE OF THE BLACK PEARL

Music by KLAUS BADELT,
GEOFFREY ZANELLI and HANS ZIMMER

Briskly

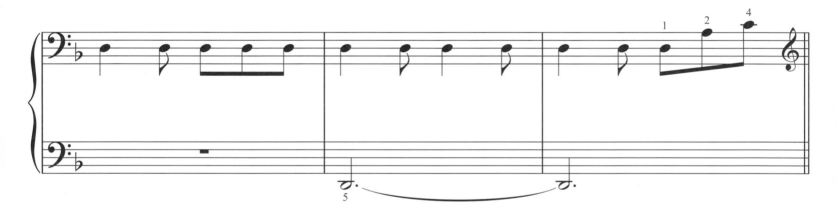

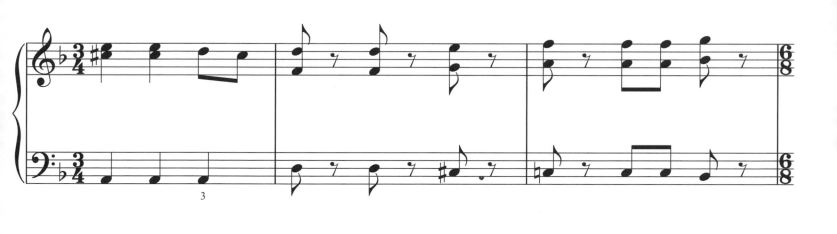

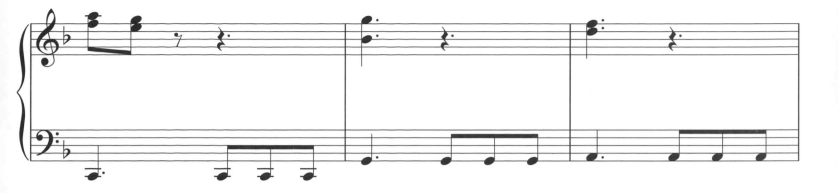

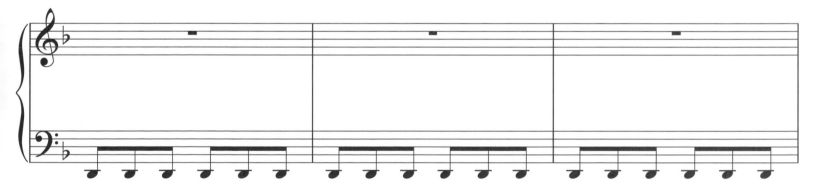

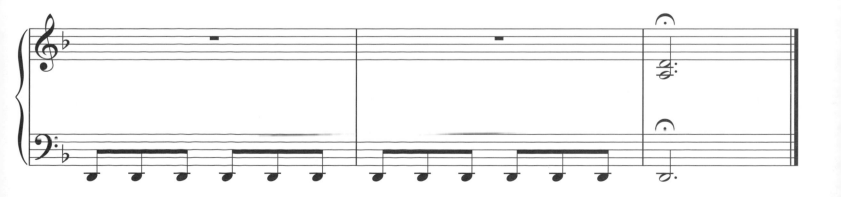

HEAVEN CAN WAIT
(Love Theme)
from the Paramount Motion Picture HEAVEN CAN WAIT

Music by DAVE GRUSIN

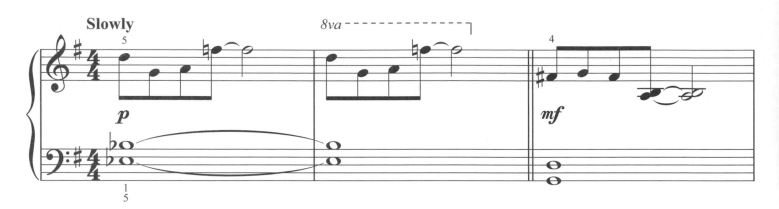

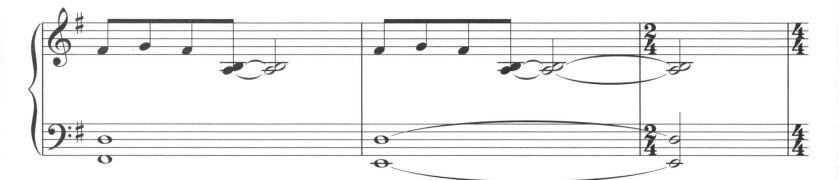

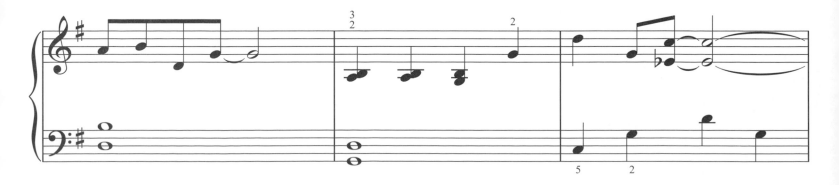

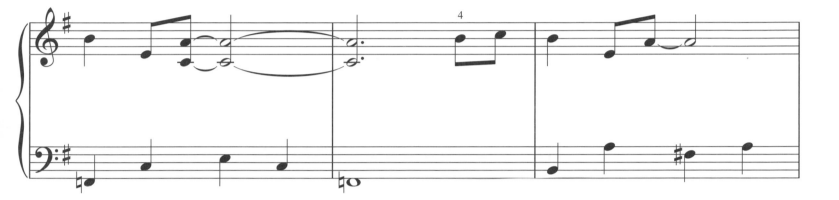

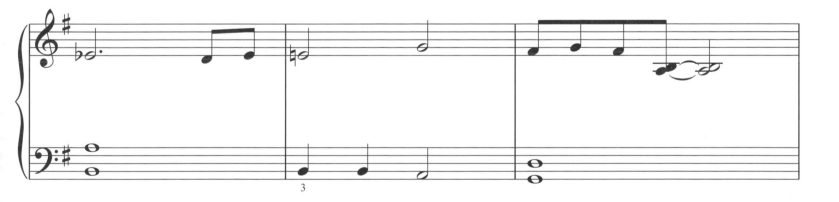

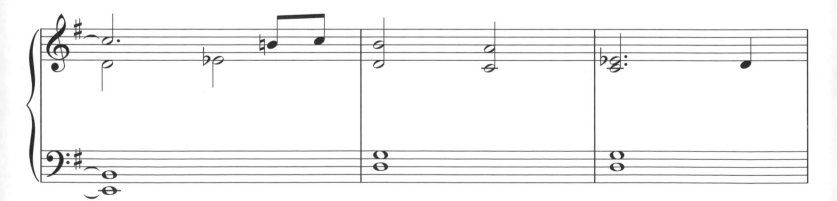

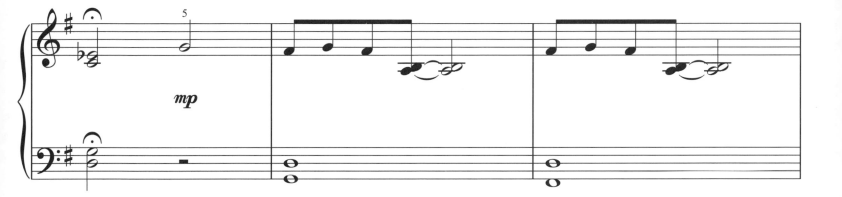

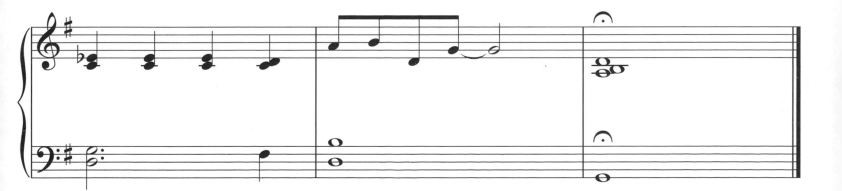

HEDWIG'S THEME
from the Motion Picture HARRY POTTER AND THE SORCERER'S STONE

By JOHN WILLIAMS

Misterioso

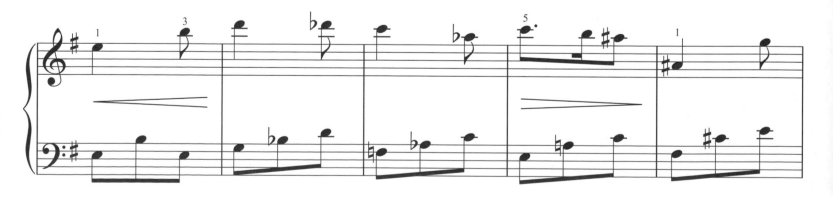

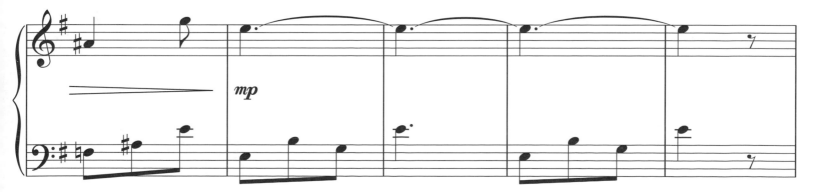

Brightly

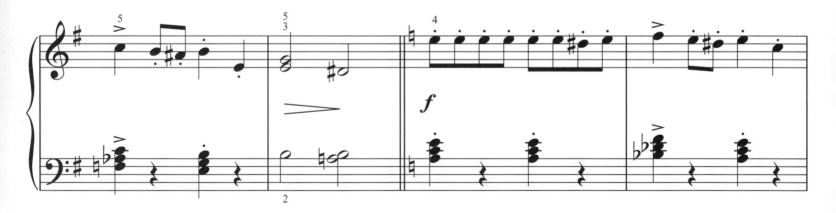

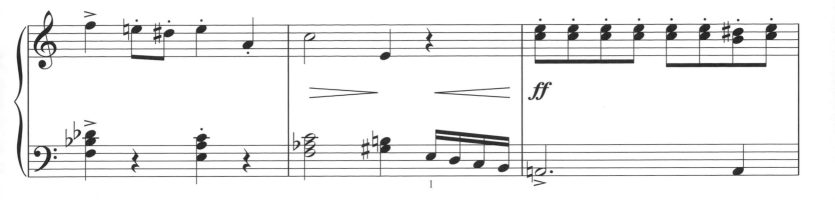

JESSICA'S THEME
(Breaking In the Colt)
from THE MAN FROM SNOWY RIVER

By BRUCE ROWLAND

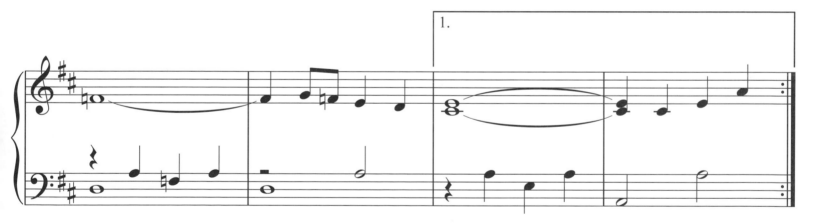

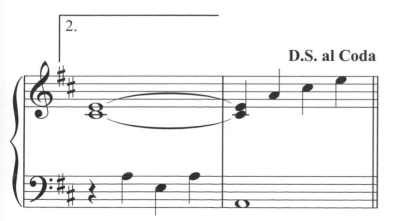

HYMN TO THE FALLEN
from the Paramount and DreamWorks Motion Picture SAVING PRIVATE RYAN

Music by
JOHN WILLIAMS

Slowly, reverently

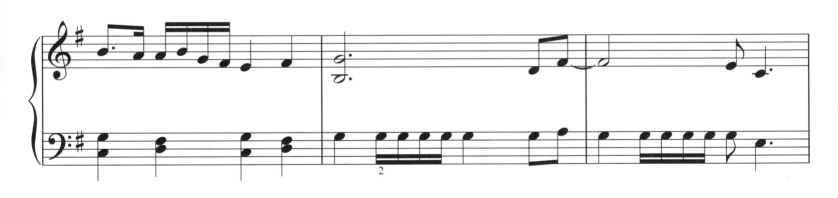

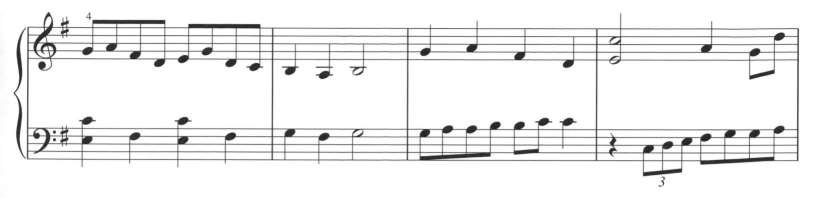

IL POSTINO
(The Postman)
from IL POSTINO

Music by
LUIS BACALOV

Moderately

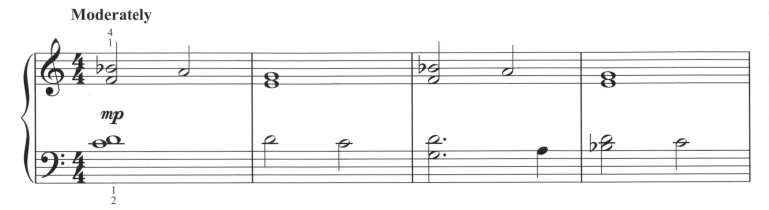

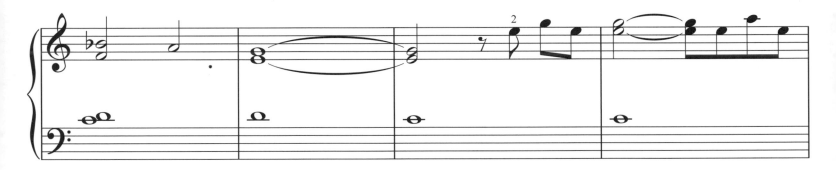

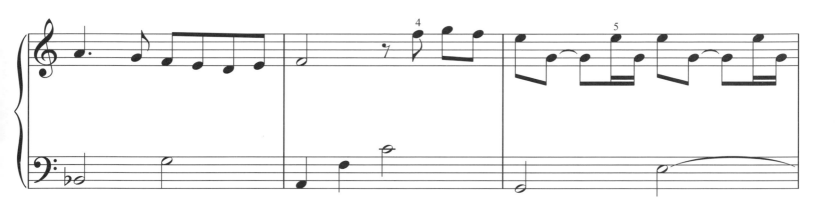

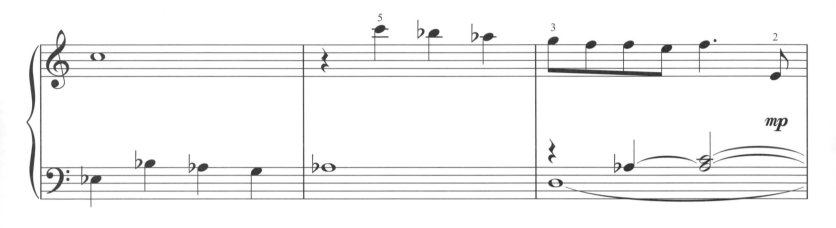

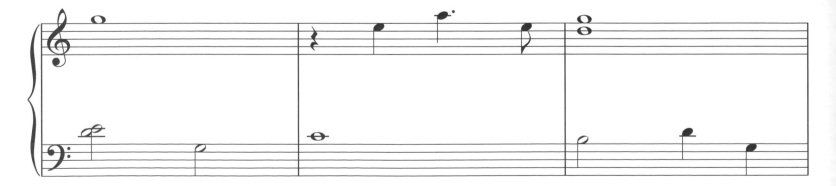

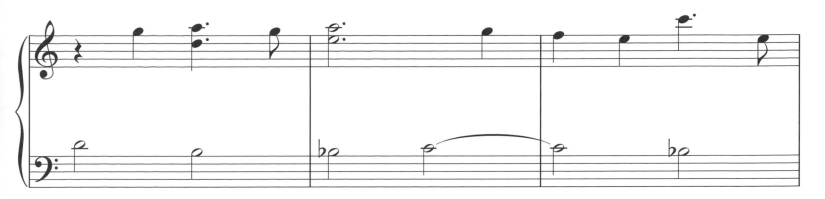

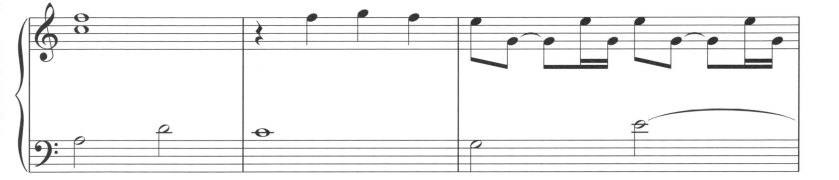

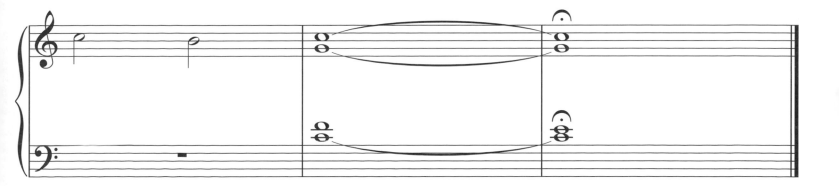

MAESTRO
from THE HOLIDAY

Music by HANS ZIMMER

Moderately

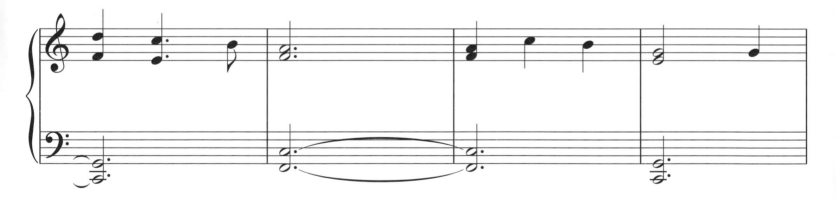

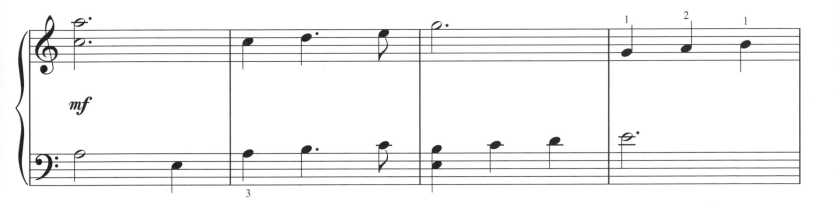

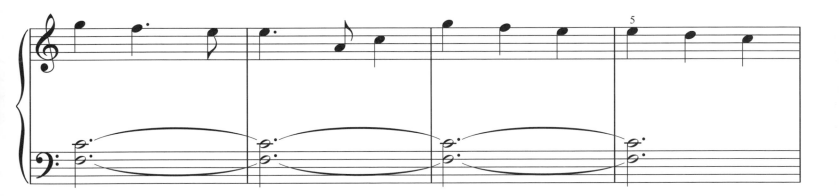

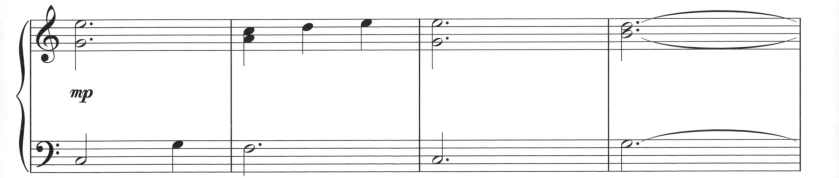

Very slowly

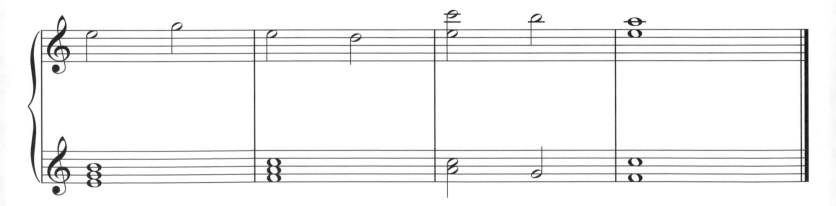

THE JOHN DUNBAR THEME
from DANCES WITH WOLVES

By JOHN BARRY

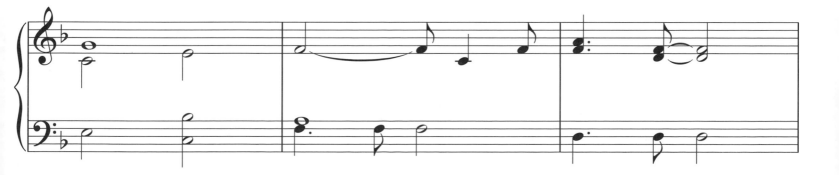

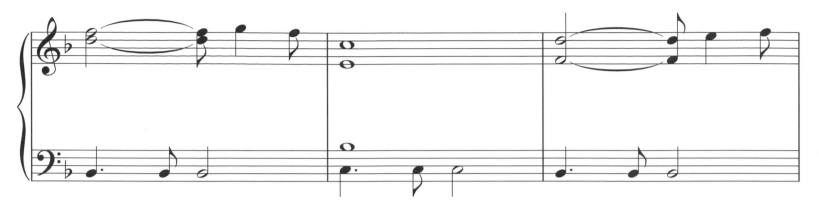

To Coda ⊕

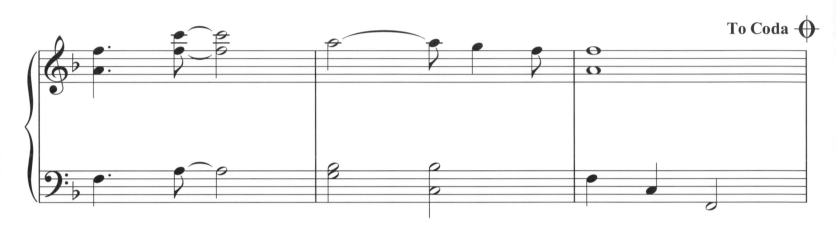

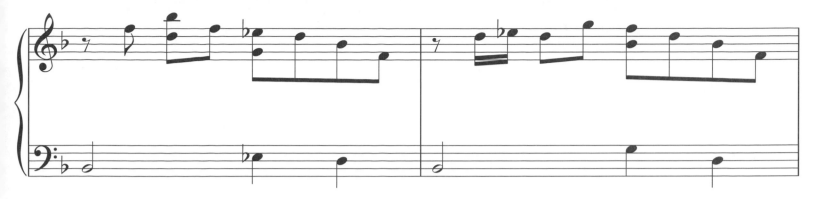

D.S. al Coda

THEME FROM "JURASSIC PARK"

from the Universal Motion Picture JURASSIC PARK

Composed by
JOHN WILLIAMS

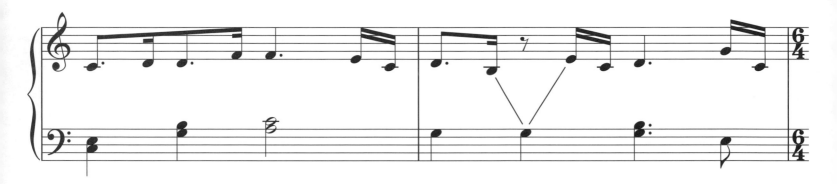

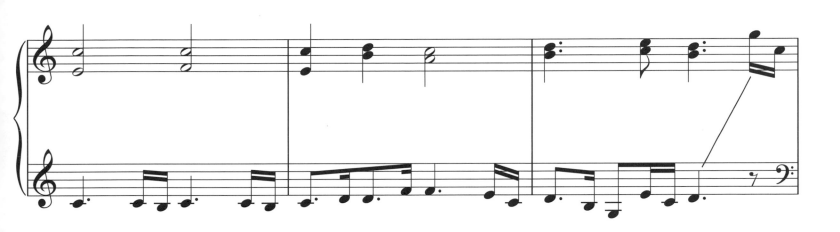

LA VALSE D'AMELIE

from AMELIE

By YANN TIERSEN

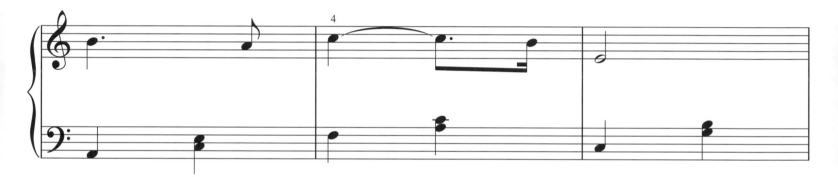

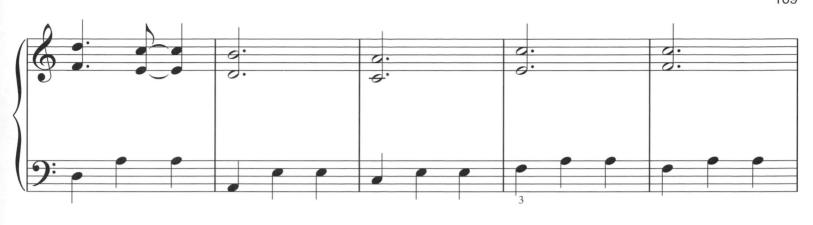

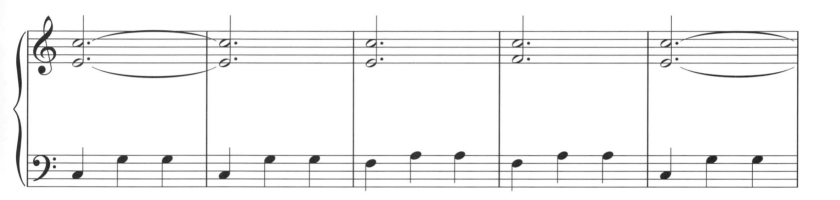

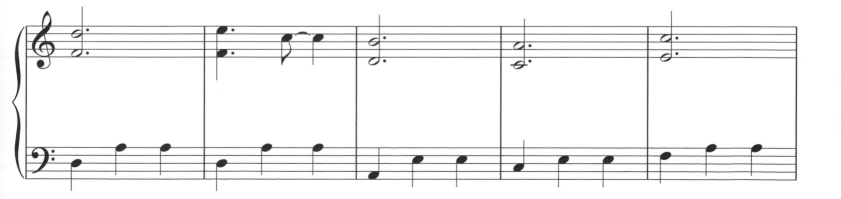

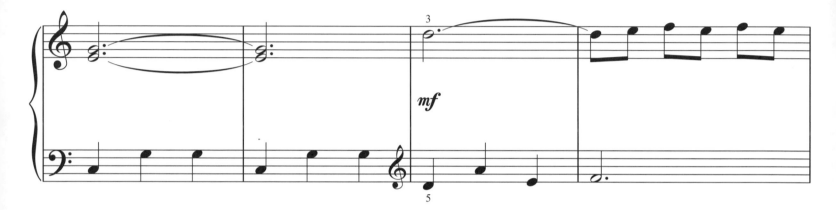

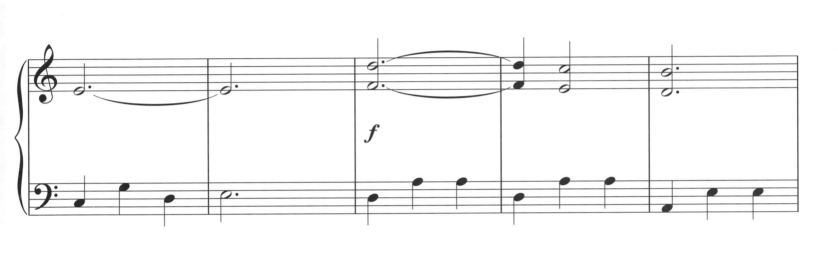

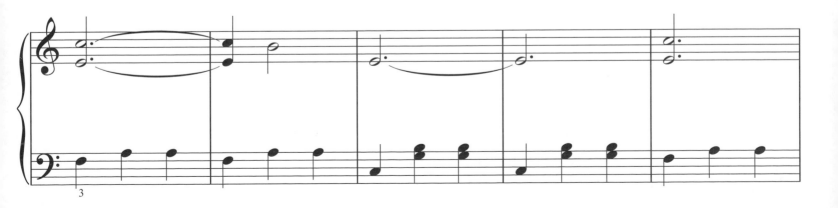

LAST OF THE MOHICANS
(Main Theme)
from the Twentieth Century Fox Motion Picture THE LAST OF THE MOHICANS

By TREVOR JONES

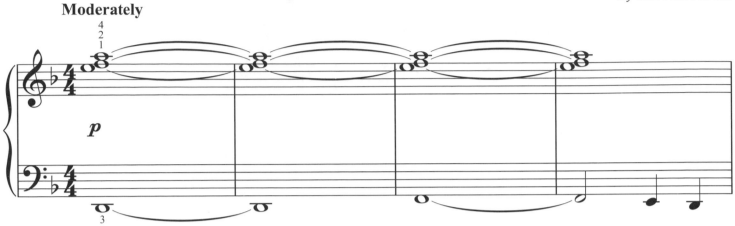

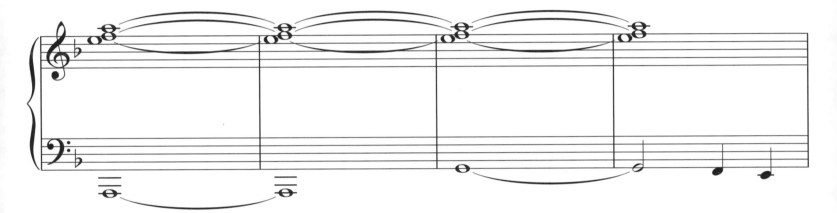

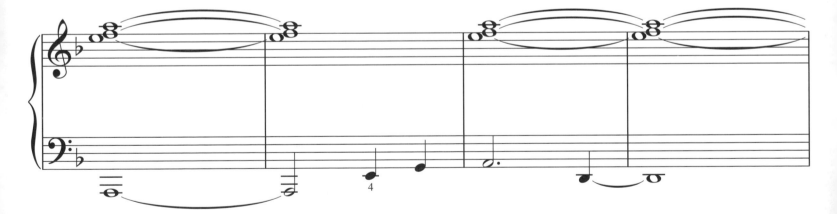

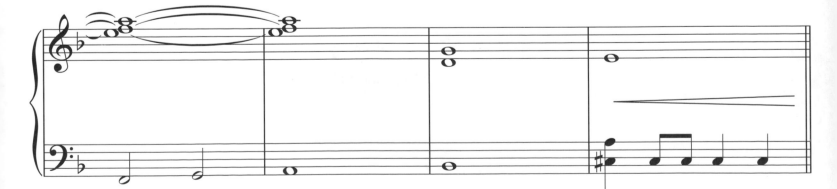

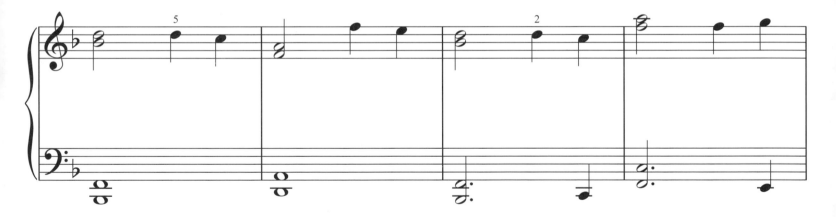

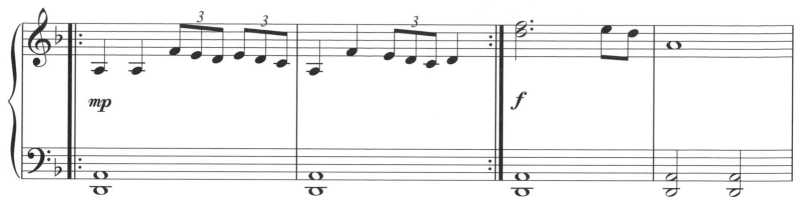

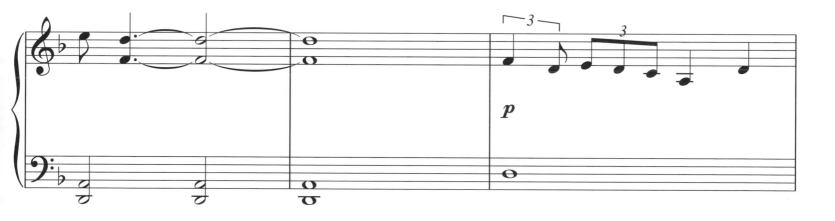

THEME FROM "LAWRENCE OF ARABIA"

from LAWRENCE OF ARABIA

By MAURICE JARRE

Slowly, with expression

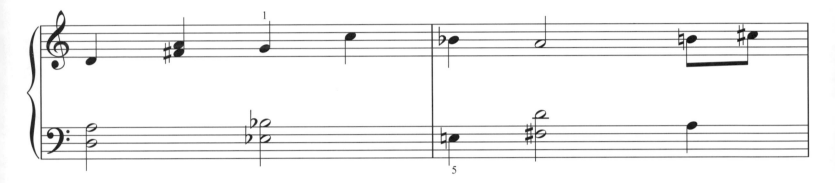

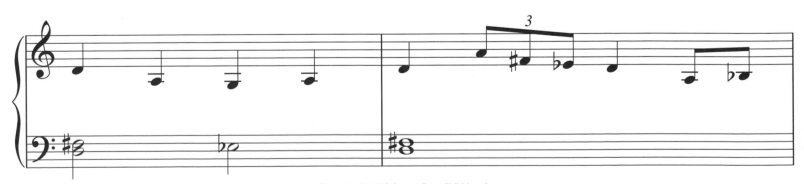

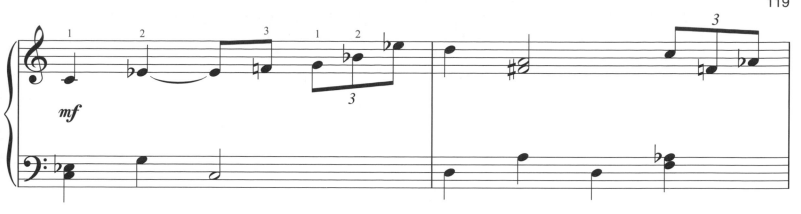

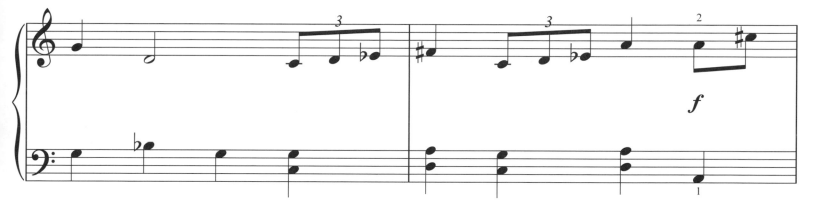

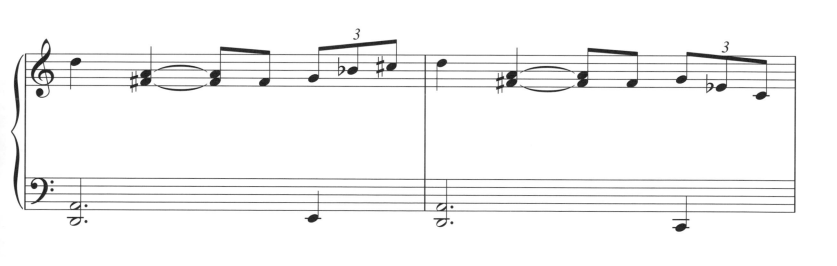

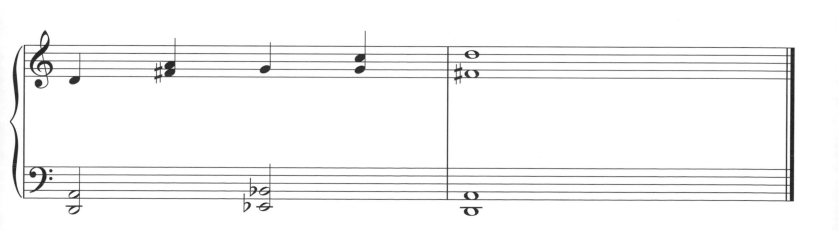

THE MAN FROM SNOWY RIVER

(Main Title Theme)
from THE MAN FROM SNOWY RIVER

By BRUCE ROWLAND

Moderately fast

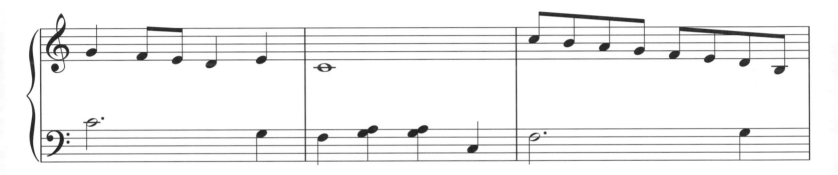

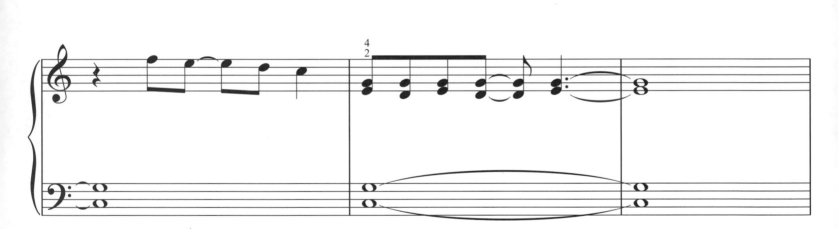

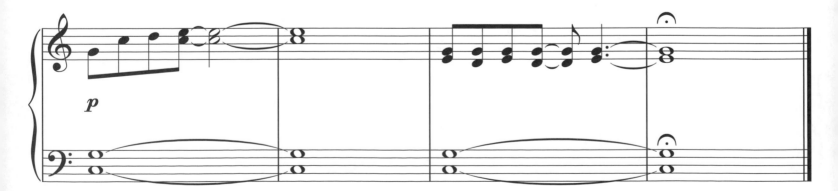

LOVE STORY
Theme from the Paramount Picture LOVE STORY

Music by FRANCIS LAI

Moderately, with expression

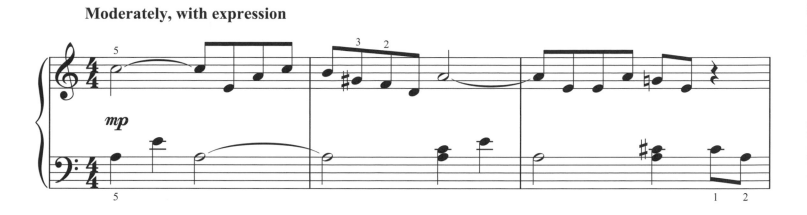

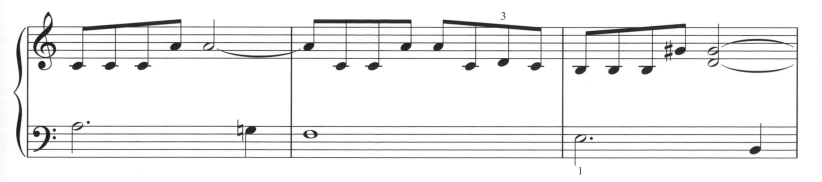

124

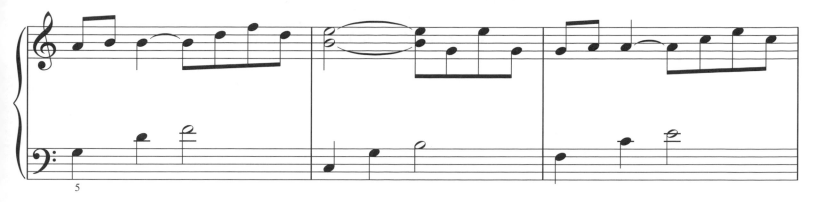

D.S. al Coda

CODA

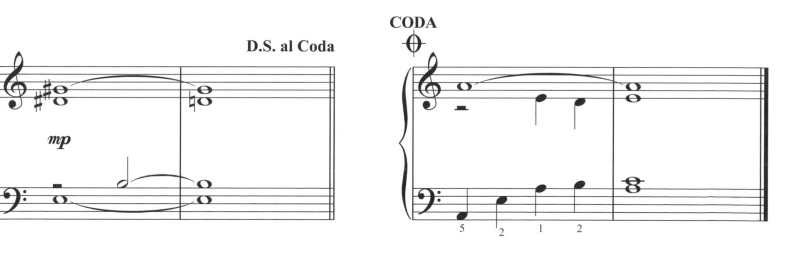

THE LUDLOWS
from TriStar Pictures' LEGENDS OF THE FALL

Composed by
JAMES HORNER

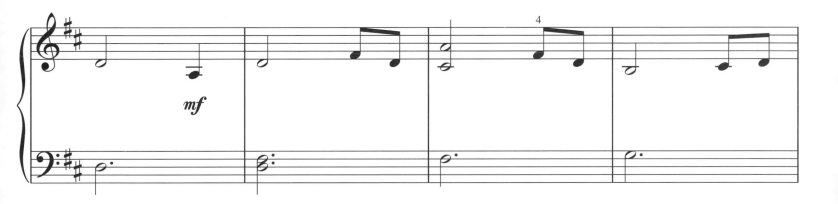

To Coda ⊕

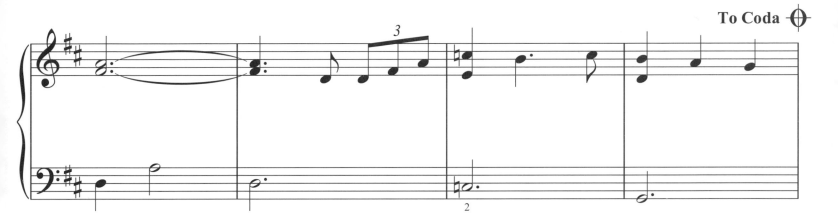

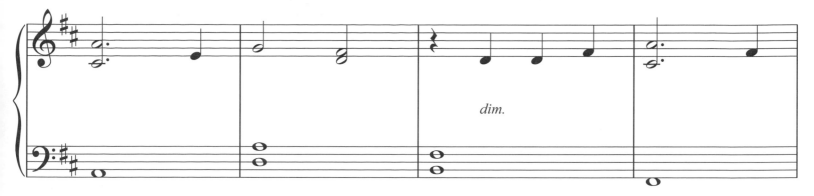

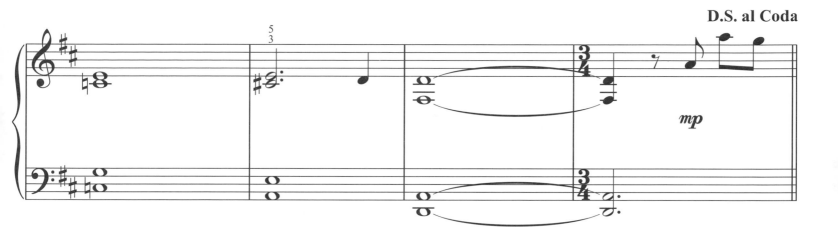

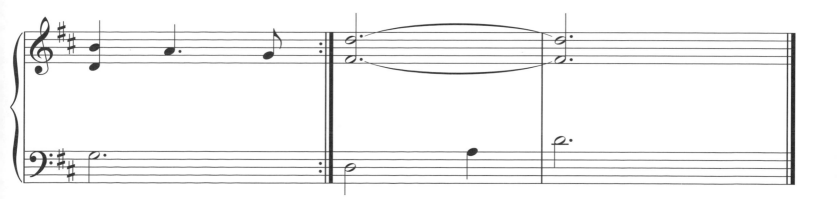

MY FATHER'S FAVORITE
from SENSE AND SENSIBILITY

By PATRICK DOYLE

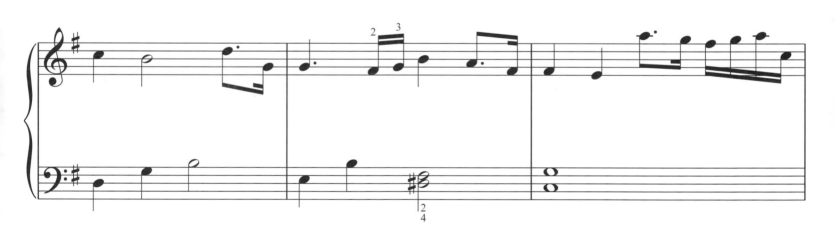

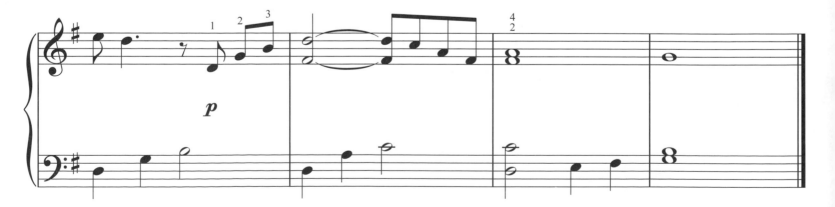

THE PINK PANTHER
from THE PINK PANTHER

By HENRY MANCINI

Moderately, mysteriously

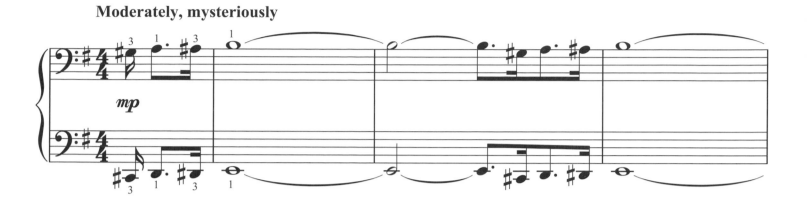

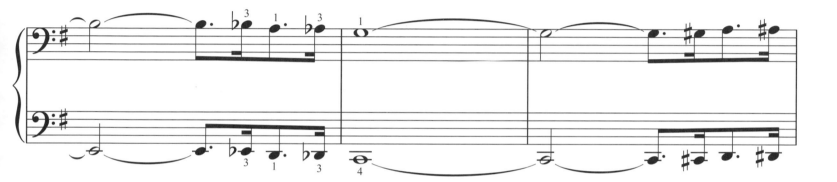

To Coda $\oplus$

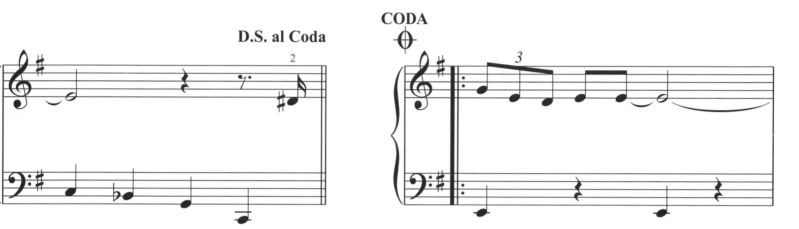

A NARNIA LULLABY

from THE CHRONICLES OF NARNIA: THE LION, THE WITCH AND THE WARDROBE

Music by HARRY GREGSON-WILLIAMS

dim.

NEVERLAND-
PIANO VARIATIONS IN BLUE
from FINDING NEVERLAND

By A.P. KACZMAREK

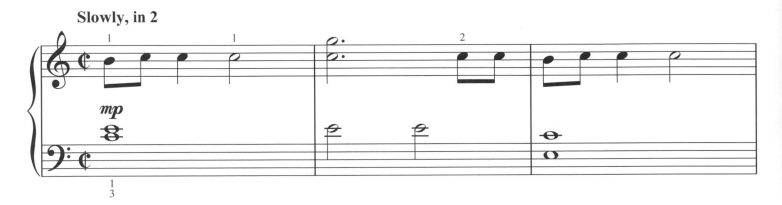

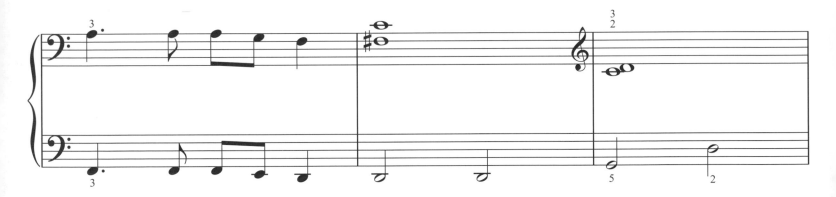

139

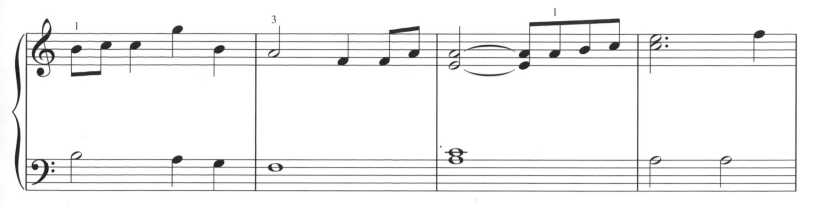

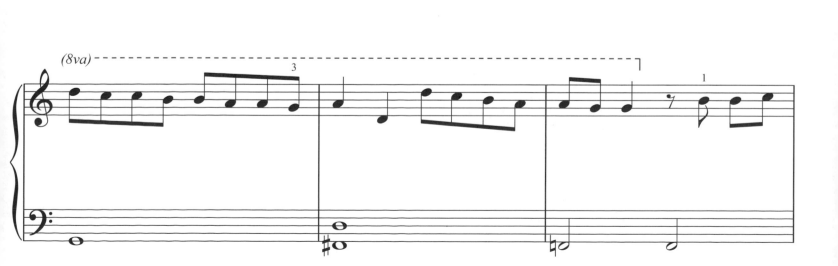

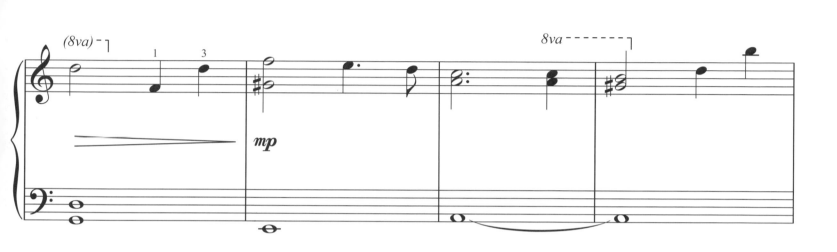

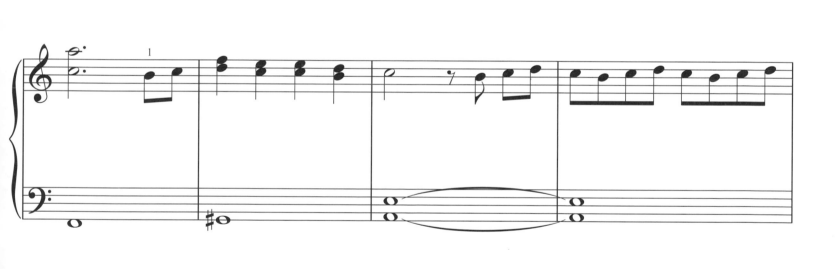

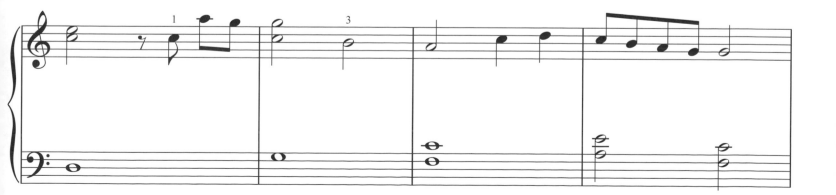

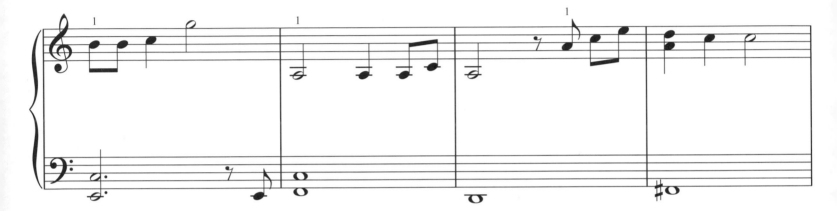

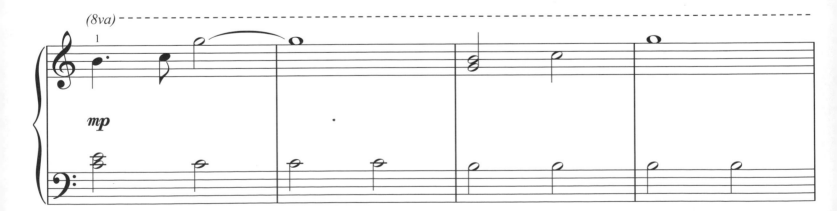

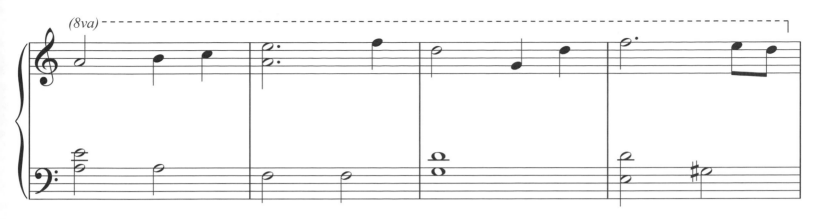

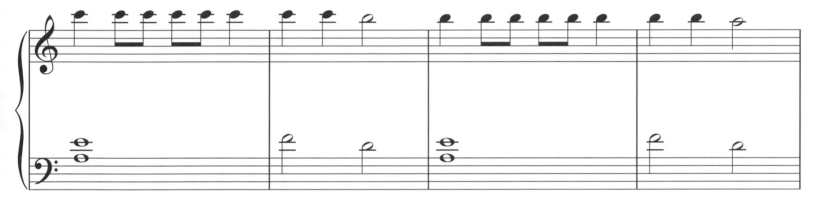

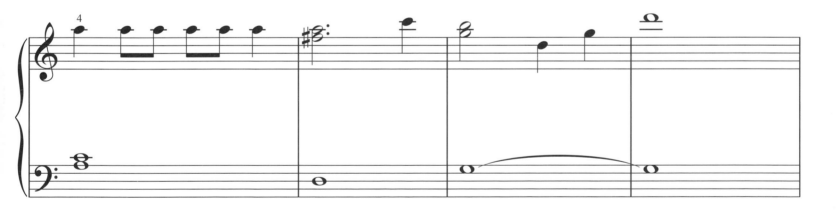

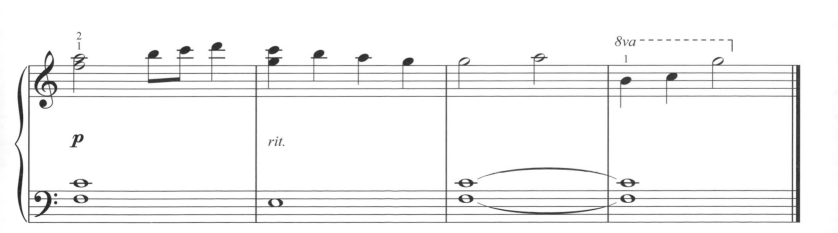

ON GOLDEN POND
Main Theme from ON GOLDEN POND

Music by DAVE GRUSIN

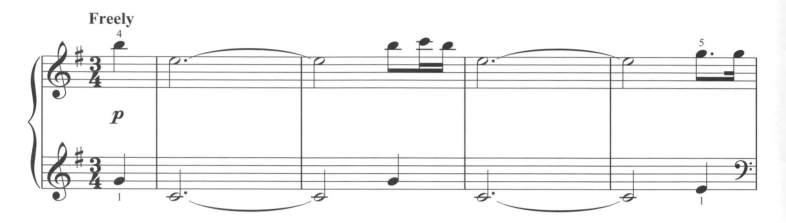

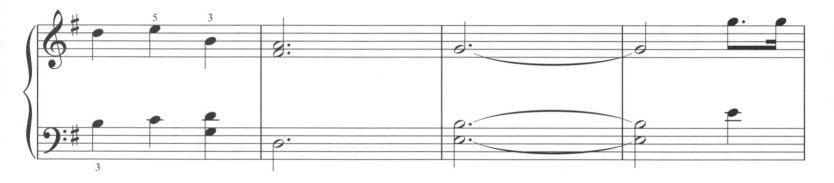

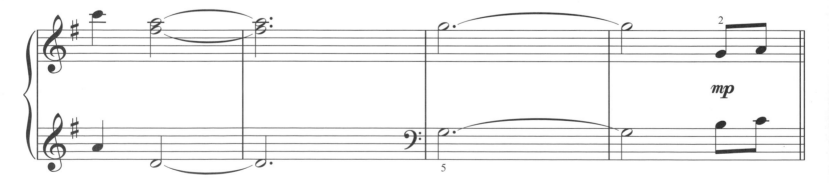

Moderately fast

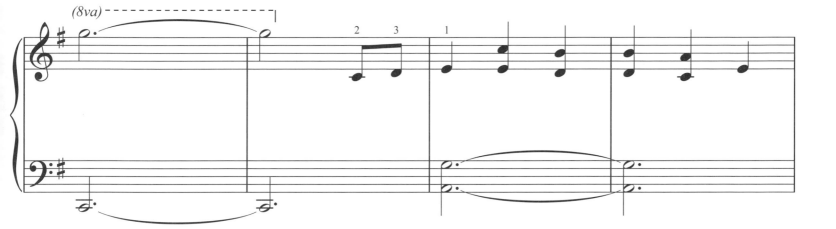

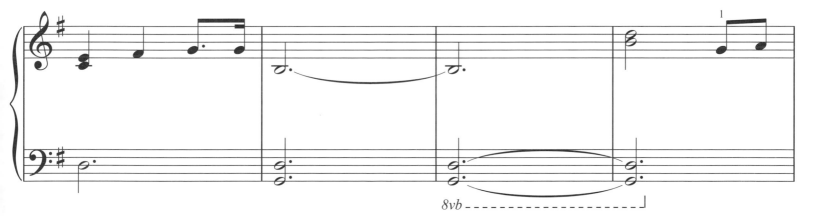

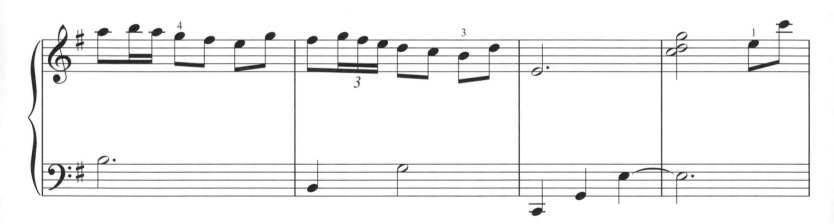

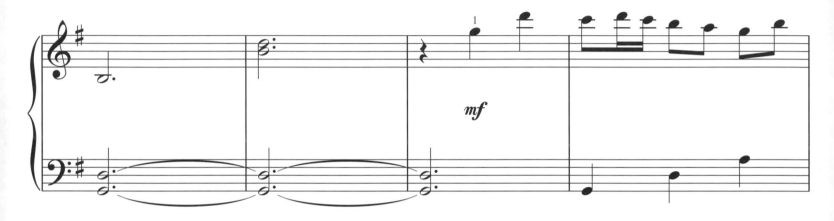

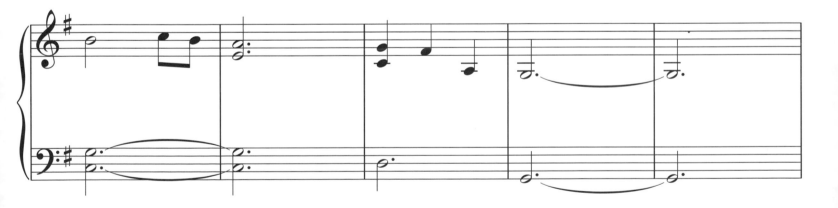

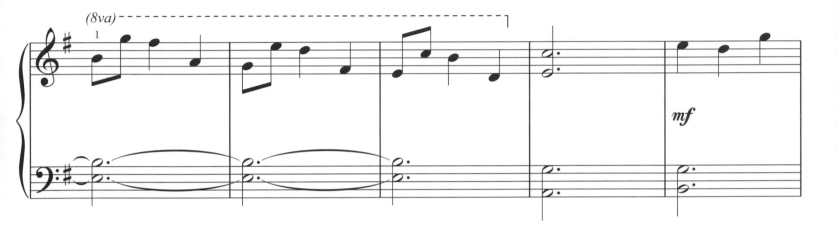

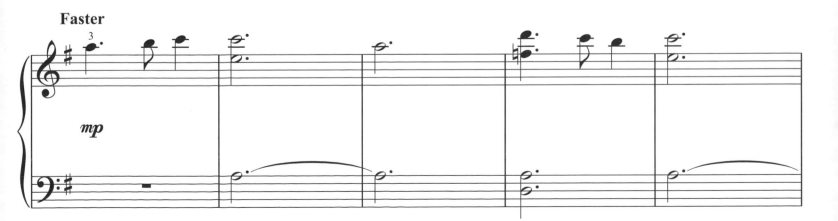

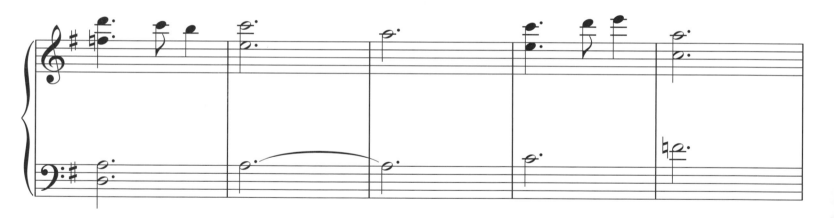

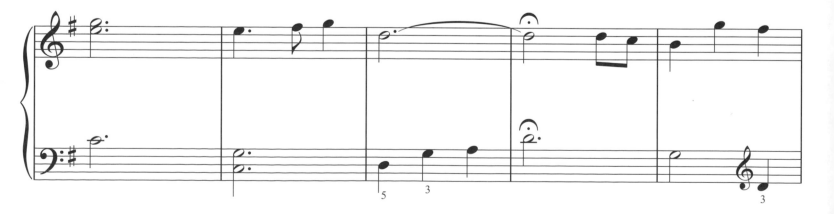

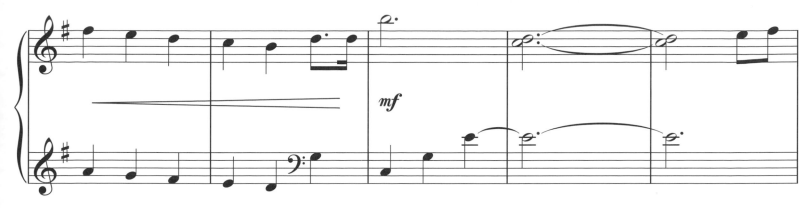

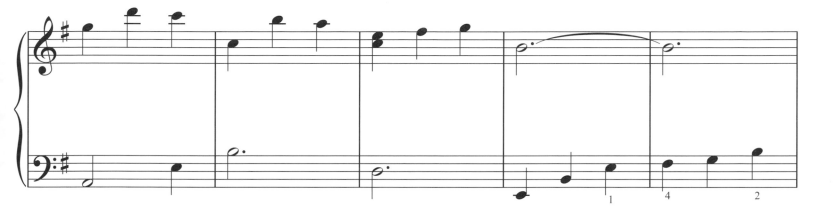

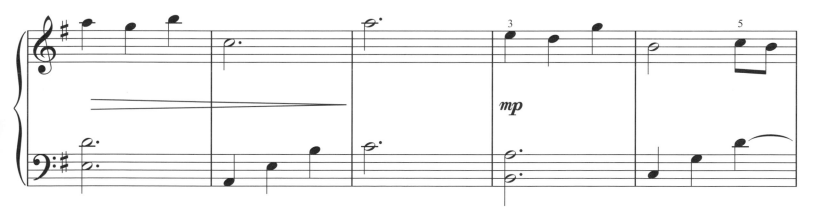

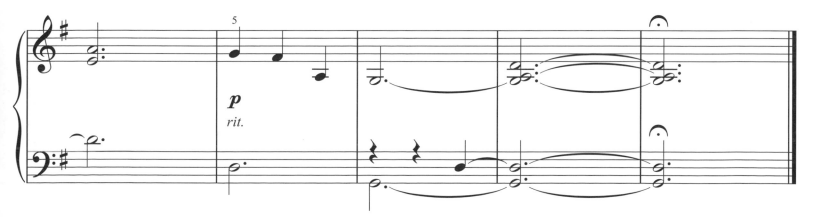

RAIDERS MARCH
from RAIDERS OF THE LOST ARK

Music by JOHN WILLIAMS

March tempo

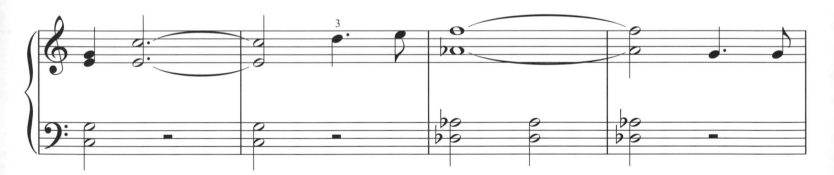

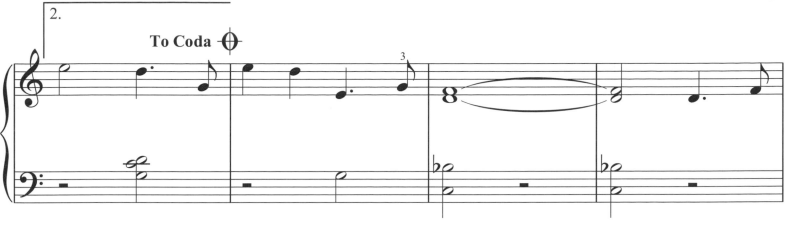

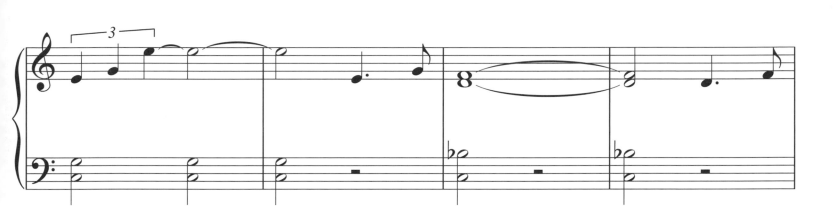

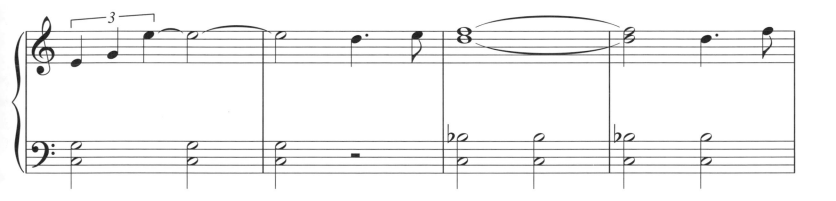

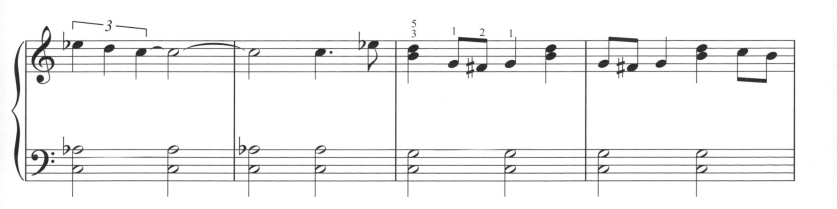

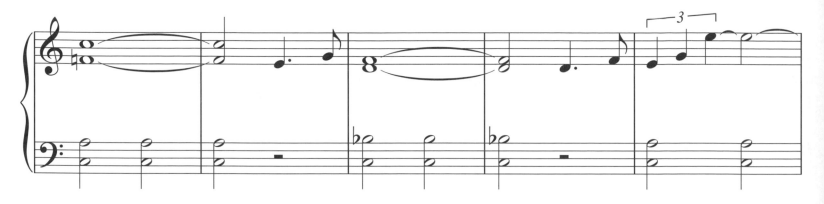

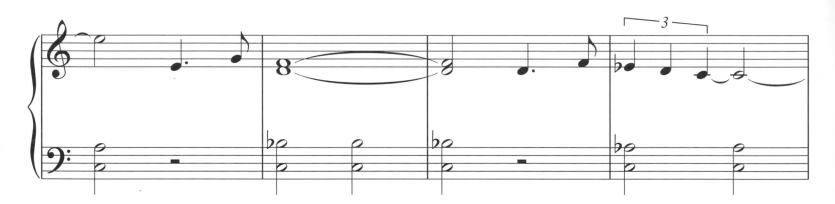

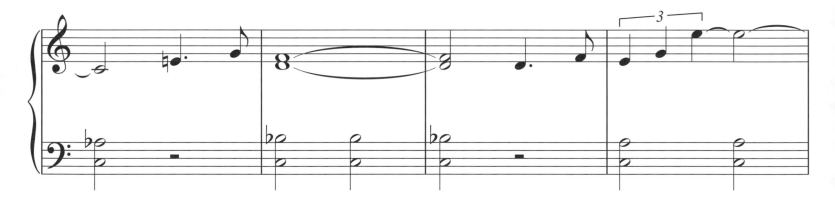

D.S. al Coda
(with repeat)

CODA

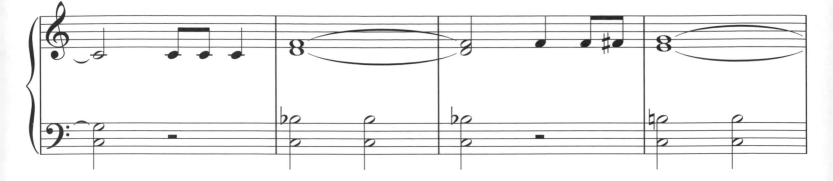

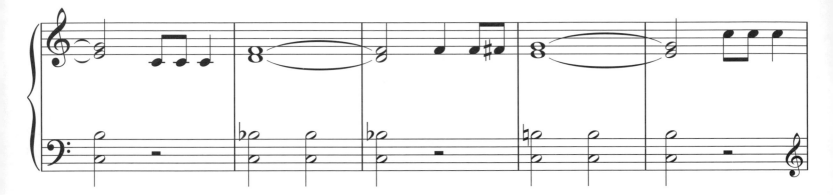

THEME FROM
"TERMS OF ENDEARMENT"
from the Paramount Picture TERMS OF ENDEARMENT

By MICHAEL GORE

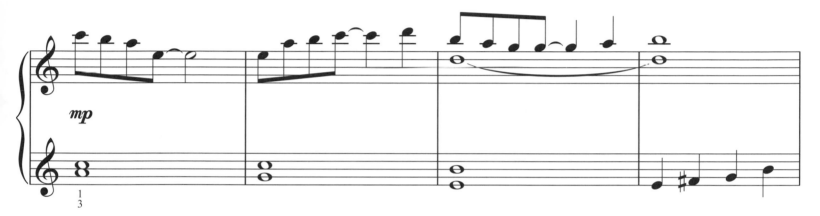

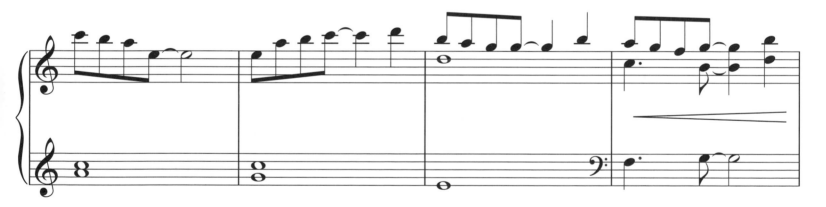

RATATOUILLE MAIN THEME

from RATATOUILLE - A Pixar Film

Music by
MICHAEL GIACCHINO

Moderately slow

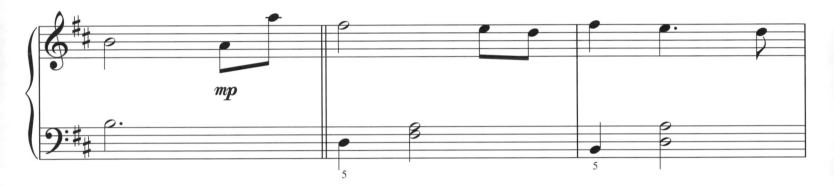

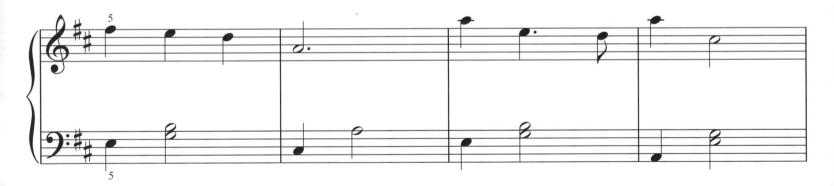

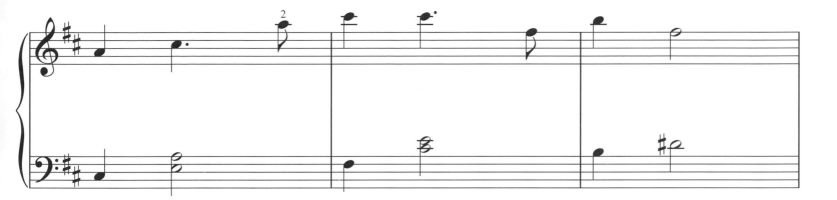

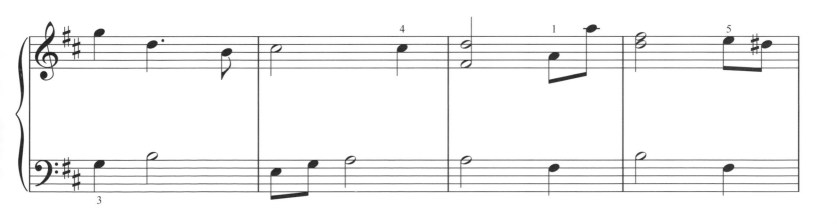

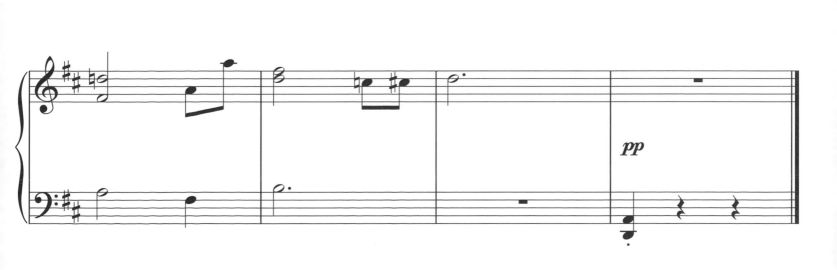

ROAD TO PERDITION
from the Motion Picture ROAD TO PERDITION

By THOMAS NEWMAN

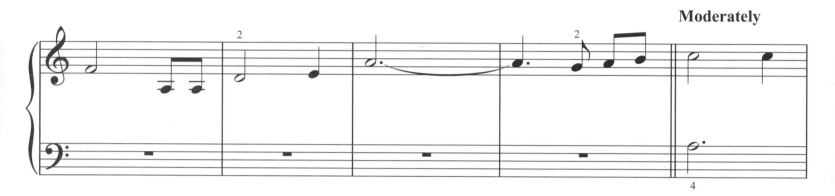

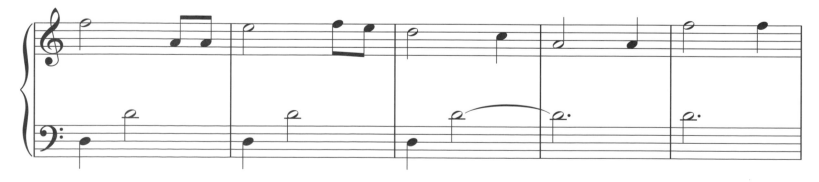

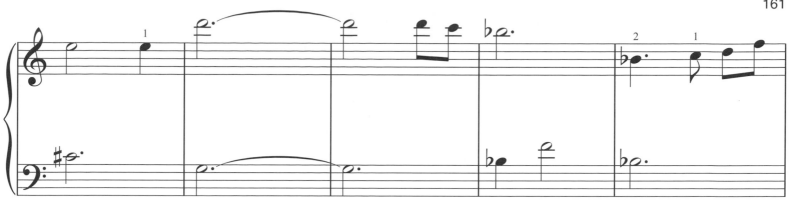

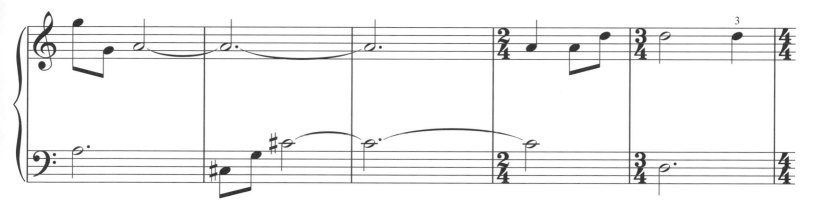

THEME FROM "SCHINDLER'S LIST"

from the Universal Motion Picture SCHINDLER'S LIST

Music by JOHN WILLIAMS

Expressively

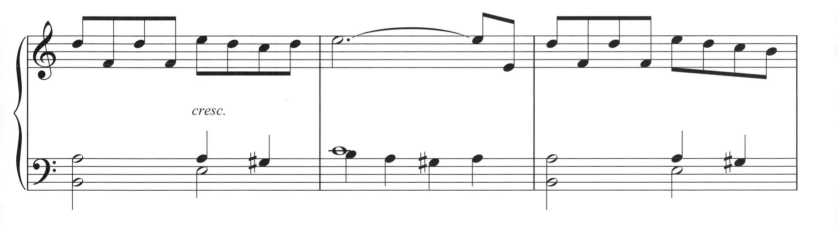

SPARTACUS - LOVE THEME

from the Universal-International Picture Release SPARTACUS

By ALEX NORTH

Flowing

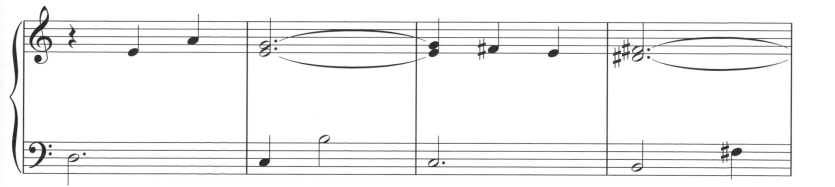

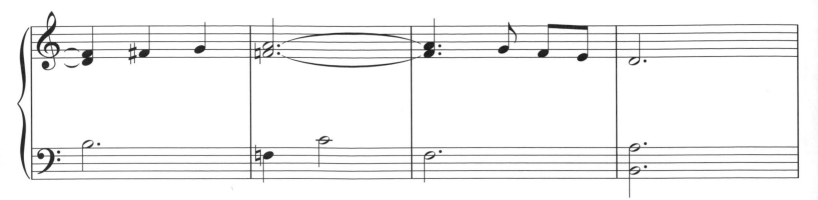

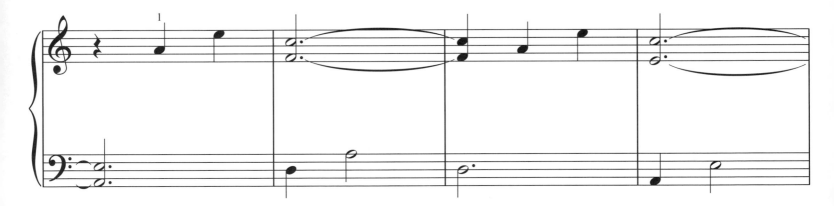

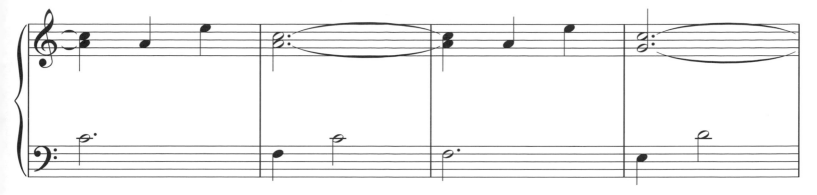

STAR WARS
(Main Theme)
from STAR WARS®: A NEW HOPE

Music by JOHN WILLIAMS

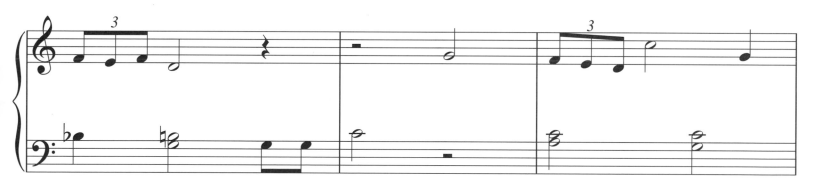

(Theme from)
A SUMMER PLACE
from A SUMMER PLACE

Words by MACK DISCANT
Music by MAX STEINER

Slowly

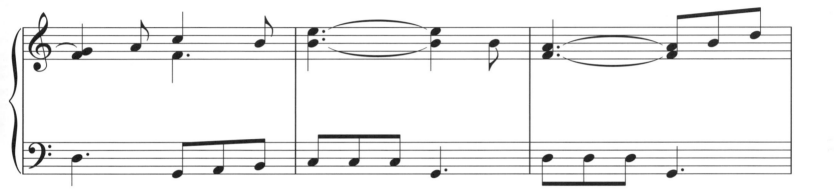

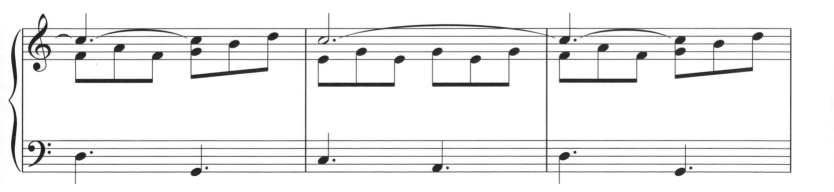

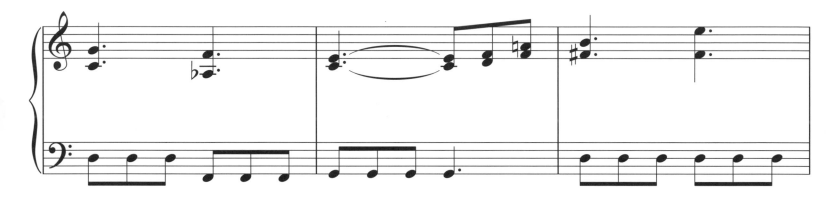

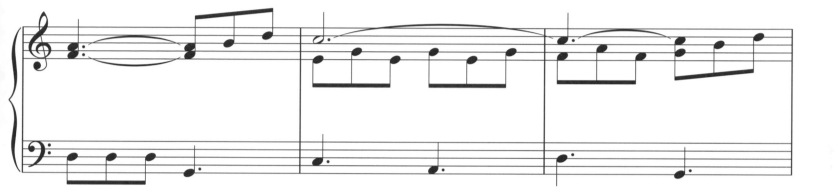

TUBULAR BELLS
Theme from THE EXORCIST

By MIKE OLDFIELD

Steadily

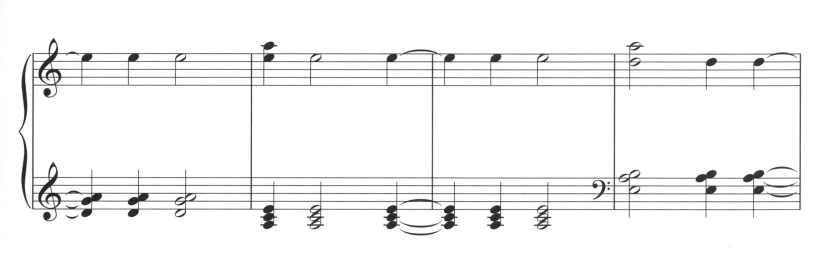

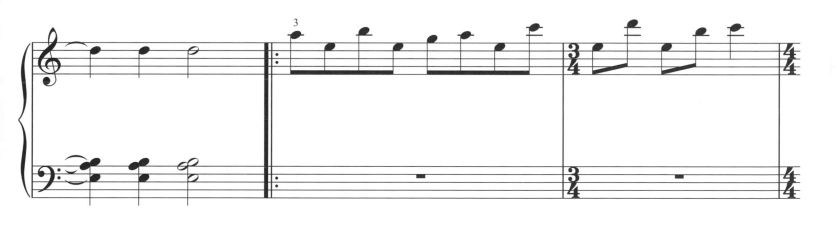

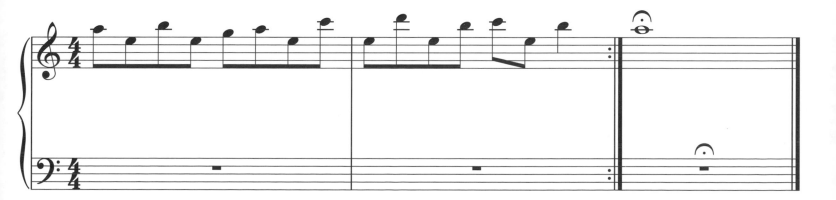

WALTZ FOR PEPPY
from The Motion Picture THE ARTIST

Composed by
LUDOVIC BOURCE

Moderately

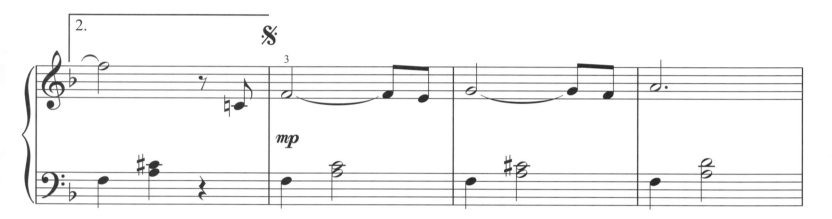

178

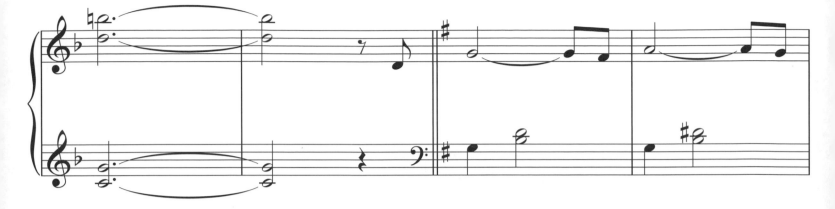

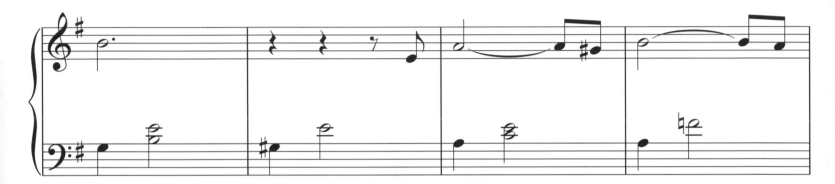

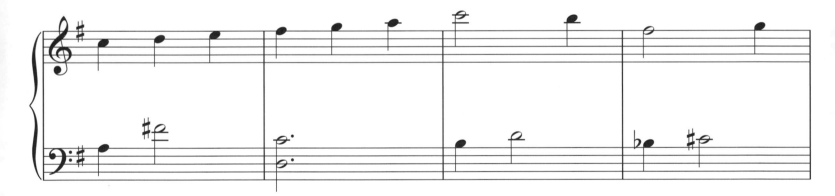

To Coda ⊕

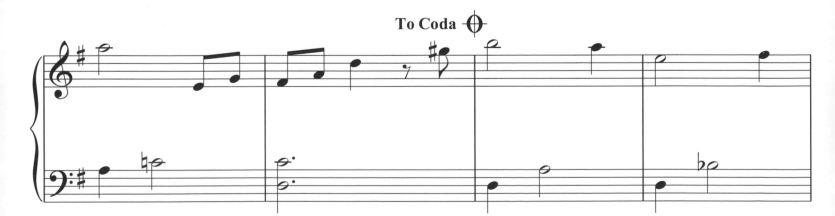

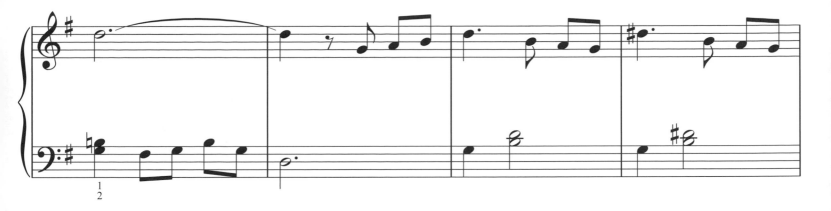

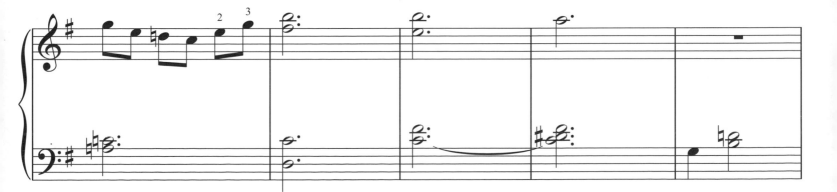

D.S. al Coda

CODA

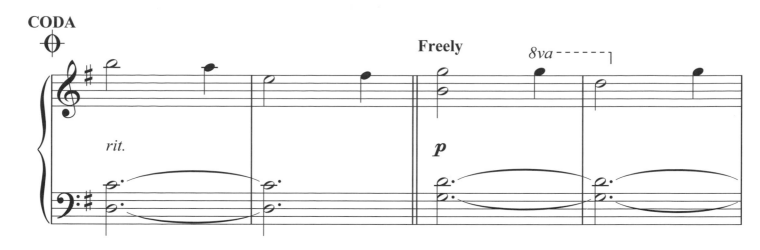

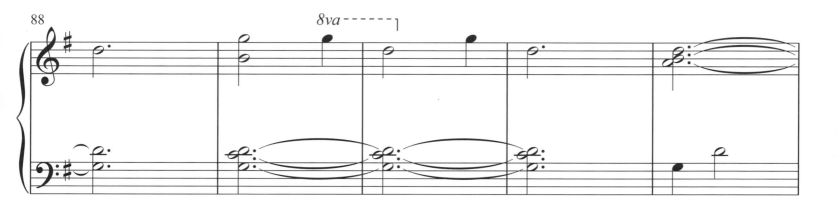

SOMEWHERE IN TIME

from SOMEWHERE IN TIME

By JOHN BARRY

Moderately slow

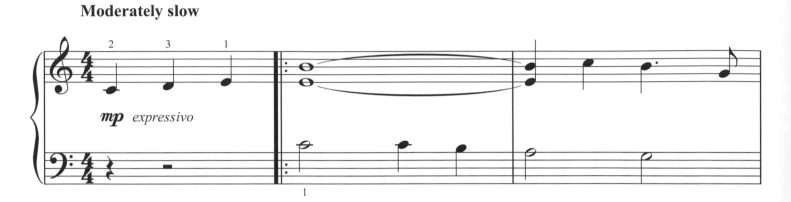

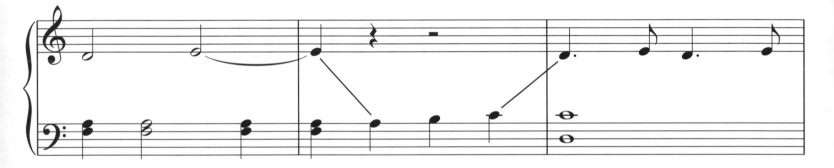

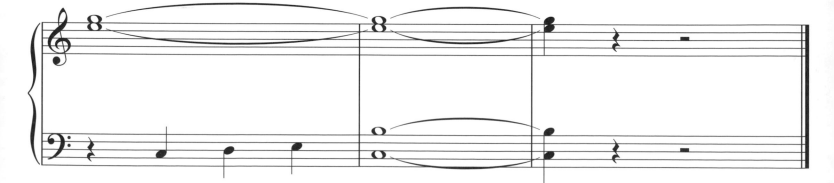